LESBIAN MOTHERHOOD:
An Exploration of Canadian Lesbian Families

The issue of gay and lesbian parenting has been the focus of much controversy in recent years. The views of politicians, the public, and the clergy have received much media attention, often overshadowing those of the parents themselves. Fiona Nelson attempts to bridge this gap with *Lesbian Motherhood*, the first study of its kind, which explores the many aspects and stages of lesbian motherhood.

Nelson's study is based on over thirty interviews with lesbian mothers in Alberta. The women fall into two groups: those raising children who had been conceived in prior heterosexual relationships and those raising children who had been conceived within lesbian relationships. The two groups provide a valuable comparison because, although the effects of the social context can be quite similar for each, their experiences of mothering are often strikingly different. Nelson explores such topics as reproductive decision-making, interacting with other mothers, the effects of the social context in which lesbian mothering is occurring, step-parenting, domestic and parenting roles, and raising boys. The non-supportive social milieu in which they exist is one of the major factors distinguishing lesbian families from many other families.

There is some discussion in the book of the political activism that has occurred in Canada around the legal status and equality of lesbian women and their families. There is also a Canadian resource directory for lesbian mothers and prospective mothers.

FIONA NELSON is completing a PhD in sociology at the University of Alberta.

FIONA NELSON

Lesbian Motherhood:
An Exploration of
Canadian Lesbian Families

21.6.96

Karen,
I'm so glad you could be
here for the book launch - and I'm
even glad you convinced me to
teach 477.
All the best,
Fiona Nelson

UNIVERSITY OF TORONTO PRESS
Toronto Buffalo London

© University of Toronto Press Incorporated 1996
Toronto Buffalo London
Printed in Canada

ISBN 9-8020-0765-1 (cloth)
ISBN 0-8020-7135-x (paper)

Canadian Cataloguing in Publication Data

Nelson, Fiona
  Lesbian motherhood

  Includes bibliographical references and index.
  ISBN 0-8020-0765-1 (bound)
  ISBN 0-8020-7135-x (pbk.)

  1. Lesbian mothers – Canada.   I. Title.

HQ75.53.N45 1996   306.874′3′086643   C95-932839-4

University of Toronto Press acknowledges the financial assistance to its
publishing program of the Canada Council and the Ontario Arts Council.

This book has been published with the help of a grant from the Social Science
Federation of Canada, using funds provided by the Social Sciences and
Humanities Research Council of Canada.

We know that all our work upon this planet is not going to be done in our lifetimes. But if we do what we came to do, our children will carry it on through their own living. And if we can keep this earth spinning and remain upon it long enough, the future belongs to us and our children because we are fashioning it with a vision rooted in human possibility and growth, a vision that does not shrivel before adversity.

Audre Lorde
'Turning the Beat Around: Lesbian Parenting 1986'

Contents

Acknowledgments

There are numerous people without whom this project would have been impossible. I owe an enormous debt of gratitude to all the women who allowed me and my tape recorder into their homes and lives. I thank them not only for participating in my research but also for providing me with an opportunity for personal growth and enrichment.

Dr Robert Stebbins was tireless in his guidance and encouragement. His kindness and wisdom were essential to the completion of this project. Thanks are also due to Dr Marlene Mackie for her encouragement and support.

Dr Eliane Silverman has been a mentor for many years. I am extremely grateful that she and Dr Leslie Miller served on my thesis-examining committee and offered invaluable advice on this project.

Several people have offered practical assistance and resources. In particular, I would like to thank Audrey Gardner for her insights during our many conversations, and Anne Erskine, Klodyne Rodney, Denise Leduc, and Mark Bilko for their assistance. Thanks also to Laura Woollard for her laughter, support, and willingness to share her thoughts on her mothering experiences. I am grateful to Janet Turner for her artwork and Caroline Wilkin for the many joys she has brought to my life. I cannot begin to thank my family for the riches they offer me. My sisters, Tara and Shannon, keep me sane and connected. My father, Blaise, is my role model of honour and integrity, and my mother, Ann, is both my dear friend and beloved foil.

Virgil Duff, at University of Toronto Press, has always been very kind, helpful and encouraging, for which I thank him. Thanks also to Sarah Robertson for her careful and insightful editing.

Finally, I thank my grandmother, Margaret Nelson. Her unwavering love, encouragement, friendship, and humour are some of my greatest sources of strength. I dedicate this volume to her.

LESBIAN MOTHERHOOD:
AN EXPLORATION OF CANADIAN
LESBIAN FAMILIES

1

Motherhood

Reproduction has changed. What was once a fairly straightforward undertaking that people either were or were not capable of has been fundamentally altered. An ideology of reproductive choice, availability of contraception, and several new reproductive technologies have combined to make reproduction something that people can consciously manipulate. We decide when or if we will pursue parenthood, and we are often able to pursue it even in the face of what a decade ago were formidable physiological or social obstacles. Definitions of what it means to have children and what it means to be a family are also changing. And, as more reproductive options open up, people who might previously not have done so are choosing to pursue parenthood. One such group is lesbian women.[1]

To explain why I have chosen to study lesbian motherhood, it is necessary to trace the evolution of my thought over the last couple of years. After having been involved in pro-choice organizations and activities for several years, I realized that the pro-choice mandate, which I had taken as self-evident, is possible only in a certain historical-cultural period. As recently as twenty-seven years ago in Canada, not only was a

1 There is debate within the lesbian community as to whether 'lesbian' should be used as a noun or an adjective when referring to individuals. I choose the usage 'lesbian woman' rather than 'lesbian' because I think with the latter there is the risk of reifying as a social category a group of people based only on their sexuality. Given, however, the politicization of lesbianism in Western society, many women are comfortable with, and claim, the reifying label 'lesbian.' Although I will sometimes use the term in this way, I more often use the term 'lesbian woman,' which I believe underscores the fact that lesbianism is a characteristic some women have in common (although its meaning varies among individuals), but not their sole identifying characteristic.

pro-choice ideology poorly articulated or elaborated, but contraceptives and contraceptive information had only just become legally available to Canadians. The issue is not whether Canadians exercised contraceptive control prior to 1969. The issue is whether an *ideology* of reproductive choice existed prior to the late 1960s. I believe that it was the beginnings of such ideas that led to the legalization of contraceptives and contraceptive information and that it was the availability of these items and services that made possible an ideology of 'choice.' One of the consequences of this new ideology is that pro-choice groups are now able to conceptualize and articulate clear mandates regarding the ideal personal, social, and cultural conditions under which to have children.

My starting point, then, was to question some of the other manifestations of the reproductive-choice ideology. An ideology originally built around techniques to *limit* and *control* the reproductive capacities of bodies now covers techniques that *extend* or *create* those capacities. Originally the idea of choice meant the choice *not* to have children at any given time. Choice now includes the choice *to* have children even if one is physiologically incapable. Reproductive technologies such as in-vitro fertilization and artificial insemination are hailed as methods to expand the choices of all people. Choice has come to refer to the right to choose when and if to have children, by whatever methods and for whatever reasons one sees fit. Choice has come to mean access both to contraceptive measures *and* to children, as desired.

While virtually anyone in Canada has relatively easy access to contraception these days, access to the other side of the choice coin, the babies, is far more limited. For those who require the cooperation of outside agencies or individuals to become parents, the options are very limited. Nonetheless, growing numbers of people who cannot 'do it themselves' feel they have a right to exercise their choice to have children and thus use all services or products that may assist them in this endeavour.

One group particularly disadvantaged in terms of such access is lesbian women. It is not that lesbian women have not always had children, it is that they have not always done it themselves, by which I mean without a direct and physical relationship with a man. The fact that lesbian women in growing numbers *are* pursuing this option is one manifestation of the ideology of choice.[2]

---

2 This is not to suggest that lesbian women never had babies via donor insemination prior to the last ten or twenty years, simply that it was not happening in the significant numbers that it is now. For further references, see the titles listed under 'Lesbian Mothering / Lesbian Families' in the bibliography.

In part, then, a study of lesbian mothers is a component of a larger project to explore the personal and socio-cultural manifestations of the ideology of reproductive choice. Lesbian women who are pursuing motherhood separate from men represent a conceptual possibility that could exist only as a part of the elaboration of the choice ideology. In this sense, lesbian women pursuing motherhood are a piece of the bigger puzzle. Still, why choose to study this piece when it would appear that the meanings and experiences of motherhood and reproduction have changed for most women? If the ideology of reproductive choice and freedom has changed what it means to *pursue* motherhood and to *be* a mother (and I believe it has), then these changes would be worthy of study and, once again, lesbian mothers would constitute only part of the larger puzzle. In this regard, however, lesbian mothers are not any old piece but in some respects may offer superior access to some of the answers I am seeking.

For example, one of my assumptions is that reproductive decision-making is a very different task today, deriving from and evoking different expectations than it did even twenty years ago, if only because the sort of planning and control available now were unavailable as recently as the 1970s. My questions then are, How do we make these decisions? How do we know when or if we do or do not want children?

Research done on reproductive decision-making among heterosexual couples (e.g., Currie 1988; Crowe 1985; Rowland 1987; Silka and Kiesler 1977) indicates that social expectations or pressures are frequently primary considerations in a couple's decision to pursue parenthood, although financial and job security are also relevant. However, research (esp. Currie 1988) also shows that a sizable portion of the heterosexual population decides not to choose in the sense that although they may or may not employ contraceptive techniques, the actual decision is left to fate.

But a lesbian woman (either single or in a lesbian relationship) who wants to have a child cannot leave the decision to fate. Further, pronatal pressures and expectations rarely influence lesbian women in the same way they influence married heterosexual women. Any woman in her twenties or thirties may feel the social expectation that she should have children. Single lesbian women or lesbian couples, however, are virtually never surrounded by family waiting for them to produce a grandchild or by friends asking when or if they plan to have children (assuming their friends and family know of their lesbianism). Not only are these expectations absent, the opposite is often true; family and friends expect lesbian women and couples not to have children. They are rarely instantly joyous and encouraging when they are told the woman or couple is expecting or has decided to have a child.

Despite these drawbacks, growing numbers of lesbian women are deciding to pursue motherhood. There is a similarity here between these lesbian women and single heterosexual women and other women who are willing to risk costly, dangerous, and intrusive technological measures (e.g., in-vitro fertilization) in their pursuit of motherhood. There appears to be some force that impels all these women to pursue motherhood despite the obstacles. But for lesbian women the social support, encouragement, pressures, and rewards simply do not exist as they generally do for non-lesbian women. My assumption is that whereas heterosexual women cite social reasons for their drive toward motherhood, lesbian women, since these reasons apply less to them, might be able to find and articulate deeper components of that desire.

Pregnancy does not 'just happen' in exclusively lesbian relationships. Every aspect of deciding to have a child and pursuing this option has to be scrutinized carefully. An additional assumption guiding this research, then, is that lesbian women may be one group that really does (or does more frequently) engage in the type of careful reproductive decision-making that is the ideal and that is increasingly expected of all women. As such, lesbian women pursuing motherhood may be most able to articulate the reproductive decision-making process of all women who face it.

It is not good enough, however, to study lesbian mothers merely because they may offer us greater insight into all mothers and into the quest for the mothering experience as it has become. The political/ideological climate that made possible the development and elaboration of an ideology of reproductive choice also makes it possible for some lesbian women to pursue motherhood by 'independent' means (i.e., outside of a relationship with a man) and for others to leave heterosexual relationships and raise their children alone or within lesbian relationships.

A new family form has become possible and must be understood on its own terms, not as an aberration or deviation from traditional family forms. It is too easy and common for lesbian mothers to be ignored in the literature on mothering or to be relegated to footnotes in the research. We must look at lesbian mothers not just because we want to know about mothering in general but also because we specifically want to understand experiences common to lesbian mothers.

'Lesbianism' and 'motherhood' tend to be regarded as mutually exclusive choices. And yet neither 'lesbian' nor 'mother' alone, even reclaimed from patriarchal discourse, can capture what it is to be both a lesbian woman and a consciously reproductive being in Canada today. Neither the discourse about mothering/motherhood nor the maternal discourse engaged in only by 'qualified' mothers has given expression to the viewpoint of lesbian mothers.

Additionally, lesbian mothers, for reasons I shall consider later, have less access to the knowledge and experiences of each other than heterosexual mothers do. Several times in the course of my research I was struck by the knowledge that I am the only person who has heard all the stories shared with me. Despite the more or less formally organized lesbian mothers' groups that exist in some urban centres, generally no more than three or four mothering couples/singles typically maintain close contact with each other (in Albertan urban centres).[3]

As my research and I have become known among lesbian mothers I have come to be regarded by some as a resource. I have at times been a conduit of information between Calgary and Edmonton and have become a sort of clearing house of information for various groups and individuals in western Canada. This clearly indicates a need within the community of lesbian mothers for greater access to each other and to each other's knowledge and experiences.

It is not good enough that lesbian (biological) mothers may participate in the maternal discourse *qua* mothers. In the same way that the tales and details of motherhood that all mothers continually share with each other seem to be vital threads holding together the tapestry of women's society, so lesbian mothers need to tell and retell, share and acknowledge, those mothering experiences that are unique to and/or common among them. Unfortunately, in response to social forces around it, the lesbian community tends to be marginalized, fractured, and insular, rendering these vital connections difficult to establish and maintain.

My 'motives' for studying lesbian mothers are thus threefold. First, it is my hope to contribute to a sociology of the family by conducting broad, exploratory research into the processes of becoming a mother and becoming a family. These processes range from the desire to have children through reproductive decision-making, to the birth and raising of the children, to the creation of the 'childed family.' Second, a sociology of the family is incomplete without an understanding of those features that are particular to lesbian families. I hope my research will offer

3 See appendix 2 for a list of contact groups in Canada.

a few answers and indicate fruitful directions for future research in this area. Third, it is my desire to contribute to the construction of a lesbian maternal discourse, to provide a link between individual women who have no access to each other, and to provide an arena where they may exchange information and share experiences.

APPROACHING THE SUBJECT

My research participants have all been mothers, and from the beginning I have felt somewhat inadequate to the task of saying anything about mothering because I myself am not a mother. A traditional sociology might find this idea laughable. It has never been seen as necessary (and rarely even preferable) that the researcher be a full-fledged member of the group she or he is studying. A feminist sociology would be more sympathetic with my discomfort and, at the very extreme, might even suggest that I can speak neither for nor about anyone anyway; that my sole responsibility as a feminist researcher is to allow the experiences and voices of women to be heard, thereby creating a place for their narratives within the academic discourse.

I do not know what portion of my discomfort has been due to my struggle to find a place for myself on the continuum of feminist sociology. I cannot know if I would have encountered this difficulty with another subject matter, another 'population.' What I have come to realize, however, is that at least part of my discomfort and hesitancy springs from the subject matter itself.

It is not terribly uncommon for men and childless women to be informed that they do not really 'know' or 'understand' because, after all, they are not mothers. As I speak with lesbian mothers I hear them say that motherhood allows them a claim to particular authority and knowledge that only mothers (lesbian or not) can have. In other words, I come up against what can be called a 'maternal epistemology.' One can claim access for oneself to this maternal epistemology only after passing certain rigorous initiation trials, which I will discuss at greater length later.

Thus I have come to realize that my discomfort and hesitancy are neither unwarranted nor mere artefacts of an adherence to a feminist agenda. My task has become to combine my own epistemology with what the women I have interviewed have to say, in an attempt to come up with something new, something true to both of us, but such that neither epistemology is allowed to dominate or veto the other.

And so something I have had to struggle intensely with during the course of this research is determining the nature of a feminist sociological epistemology and making it work for me. I have approached this question as if an epistemology were something one could shop for and 'put on' when the most pleasing version was found. While a part of me has agonized over an exploration of epistemologies, another part has interviewed women, formulated thoughts, and discussed them in what has turned out to be a fascinating discursive process.

I have come to the realization that neither was I without an epistemological stance nor was I employing some sort of neutral epistemology to guide my inquiry until I found an acceptable epistemology with which to proceed. Certainly, I would contend that my epistemological capacities have been given a broad structure by both feminism and sociology, but in the final analysis I am an individual who is situated socially, culturally, and historically within my unique life, and these factors constitute my epistemology.

It is not surprising therefore that another area of struggle for me has been to situate myself in my research (maintain cognizance of my 'motives') and also to situate my research in my life. This has been a recursive process and so can be thought of or discussed only circularly. But I knew from the beginning that my research ran parallel to an internal process that also preceded it. I assumed that it had something to do with my own decision-making regarding whether to pursue motherhood. Even so, I was surprised to realize well into my research that some of the questions I was pressing the most were the ones I have not been able to answer satisfactorily for myself. I wanted to know how other women answered these questions.

I have come to realize that what I thought on a personal level was about becoming a mother was more about mothering in general. Whereas I set out to explore how the concept of motherhood manifests itself socially and how individual women actually experience it, I did not for a long time look at my own investments in the idea. It was as if by being a non-mother I could be more 'objective' about motherhood. But none of us is immune to mothering. I am reluctant to admit that it took me a long time to realize that I cannot separate the concept of motherhood from mothering as I have experienced it, just as I cannot completely separate the mothering I receive from the mothering I give or may give in the future.

It cannot be irrelevant to my approach to this research, or to my thoughts about what women have said to me or to how I organize my findings, that I hold mixed feelings about the mothering of which I have been the recipient. In facing common ideals about the strength, unique-ness, and transcendency of 'mother love' I find myself sceptical. I would imagine that some of the women I have interviewed would not be com-pletely comfortable with my scepticism.

Of course, it is not at all uncommon to be dissatisfied with one's mother or with the mothering one is receiving or has received. The 1990s may well be the decade during which we will all realize that we come from 'dysfunctional' families. This claim is one I have encountered so often, both in my research and in my daily life, that its significance cannot be ignored. By the same token, I have encountered it so often that its meaning has begun to blur. My point in bringing this up is to indicate that my respondents, myself, and my entire research project exist along-side (although not independent of) various popular ideas and ideologies regarding motherhood and the family.

Additionally, my respondents and I, as members of the lesbian and gay community, have developed great wariness of researchers and their research. I am repeatedly challenged to explain *why* I am studying les-bian women and *what* I intend to do with the information. The caution is understandable because the risks are real. I would argue that research (social scientific, psychiatric, and medical) has played a decisive role in *creating* gay and lesbian people as a distinct population (or populations). Research has tended to start from the often implicit assumption that such a population does exist, different and separate from the rest of soci-ety, and that this population, or portions thereof, can be isolated and studied to afford the rest of *us* greater insight into *them*. Such research, sometimes even intended to enlighten the population at large or arouse 'sympathy,' serves to reify the categories of 'gay males' or 'lesbian women' as *actual social artefacts* that are accessible to the researcher and yet still somehow alien to the common person.

The other extreme is not to identify gay and lesbian people as distinct groups, in fact not to identify them at all. The tendency here is to formu-late broad paradigms based on heterosexual (and usually white and middle-class) experience and simply assume that everyone else fits in. This strategy renders invisible and inaccessible to consumers of the research those experiences of other groups that *are* unique to them.

The tenuous middle ground between these two extremes revolves around the idea/reality of 'experiences.' Specifically, there are some dif-ferences in experiences between the heterosexual population and the homosexual population, and these differences are frequently meaning-ful enough to make life as a lesbian woman different from life as a heterosexual woman and some of the specific rewards and challenges known to lesbian mothers different from some of those known to non-lesbian mothers.

It is never my intention to suggest that lesbian mothers encounter a wholly different experience of motherhood. I believe that what could make mothering and motherhood fundamentally different experiences for different women are very broad cultural and historical differences between them. And, within the same historical era or cultural milieu, it appears that economic and ethnic factors make for greater differences in how motherhood is experienced and understood than the sexual orientation of the mother possibly could.

THE STUDY

Between February and August of 1991 I interviewed thirty lesbian women in Calgary, Edmonton, and Lethbridge, Alberta. I first advertised for respondents in September 1990. For over five months my ads ran in lesbian publications, were distributed at social events, and were posted in gay/lesbian clubs and restaurants. That it took so long to gain access to my sample population reveals some interesting characteristics of that population, on which I will elaborate in my discussion of the sample.

I contacted a couple of women who were members of a lesbian mothers' group and spoke to them about my research. Since no one ever responded to my ads, the entire sample was gathered by the snowball method, by which respondents referred me to other respondents, starting with these women.

My plan was to interview each individual woman and, in the case of couples, also interview the couples together. I was able to interview all the individuals but sometimes it was impossible to meet again with the couples. I participated in a total of thirty-four interviews, ranging in length from forty-five minutes (with couples) to four and a half hours (with individual women).

I had devised a general interview schedule (see appendix 1), which served primarily to remind me of the main areas I wanted to discuss with the respondents. Apart from this guide the interviews were relatively unstructured. I would frequently allow the talk to follow the usual roundabout pattern of normal conversation for a period of time, fitting in my questions where appropriate and sometimes pulling us back on track if we digressed too much.

The major areas for discussion included in my interview guide were reproductive decision-making and the experiences of becoming pregnant, giving birth, and creating a family. As the interviews progressed there began to emerge other important topics (e.g., the striking presence and influence of a culture of 'mother talk'), which I pursued with later respondents. Having reached the saturation point with some of the standard questions I had focused on earlier, I felt comfortable giving them less emphasis (though not omitting them) and diverging somewhat from my interview schedule.

The fluidity that I sought in the individual interviews was thus also a characteristic of the research process itself. As patterns and ideas occurred to me I was able to discuss them during interviews. This provided a reassuring check for me and on occasion required me to rethink my generalizations if respondents indicated that a formulation of mine did not quite ring true for them.

All the interviews were tape-recorded, with, of course, the women's consent. Most of the interviews were conducted in the respondents' homes, a few in my home, and one in my office at the university. This choice again was left completely to the respondents. I wanted them to choose the place that was most convenient for them or where they felt most comfortable.

I was frequently asked to explain my research and sometimes, somewhat suspiciously, to justify my motives. Although sometimes difficult to answer, these questions served the vital purpose of requiring me to continually formulate and reformulate my thoughts on the project and explore my own motives so that I could answer in a truthful and knowledgeable way.

As I transcribed the interview tapes I struggled with the question of how close to verbatim the transcripts should be. Did I need to include 'ums,' 'ahs,' 'you knows,' pauses, laughter? I was distinctly uncomfortable about leaving anything out and so, for the most part, my transcripts are as close to verbatim as possible.

The agonizing I did over how to transcribe is not a minor or merely technical concern. Feminist researchers, especially those engaged in linguistic and conversation analysis, contend that what women do not or cannot easily express can be as revealing as what they do say. Devault (1990), for example, argues that 'ums' and 'ahs' can be important indicators of women struggling to express their subjective experiences with the language that is available to them. It is at these points that we should be particularly attentive to what is being talked about. She contends further that the phrase 'you know' may not be for women the filler or link-ing device that conversation analysts tend to see it as. She argues that 'in many instances, "you know" seems to mean something like, "okay, this next bit is going to be a bit tricky. I can't say it quite right, but help me out a little; meet me halfway and you'll understand what I mean"' (1990:103). It might also be an attempt by the speaker to determine whether the listener shares her point of view.

If we accept the feminist premise that women are trapped in a male language that sometimes inadequately conveys female experience, we can see how important it is to take special note of these moments of struggle. It is also clear how omitting such moments from transcripts might be equivalent to throwing out some of the most telling pieces of information. My project here is not a conversation analysis and so I rarely discuss these moments, but I strove to remain sensitive to them as I read the transcripts and listened to the tapes.

Another concern for me, as a feminist researcher, is what to write and how to write it. I feel it is necessary that the women who spoke with me be, at least, as present here as I am. I have thus designed my presenta-tion to fit like a frame around their voices. I have given the women pseudonyms, both to organize their voices and to preserve confidential-ity. Apart from the pseudonyms, however, no individual identifying information is given about any of the women. I will relate the rationale for this more fully in my discussion of the sample.

As important as it is for the women to be present here, it is as impor-tant for me to be present as well. A traditional formal style of writing would have me never refer to myself, perpetuating the illusion that the truth objectively exists and that *any* properly trained observer can accu-rately apprehend it and impersonally convey it, thus rendering the iden-tity or presence of the researcher superfluous.

This style would also require, if I found it absolutely unavoidable to refer to myself, that I do so as 'the (impersonal, disembodied) researcher.' But I am not just 'the researcher.' I am a white, middle-class lesbian woman who was welcomed into other lesbian women's homes, drank their tea, played googly-games with their babies, shared my own process of deciding whether and when to pursue mother-hood, and was lucky enough to be invited to a couple of lesbian-mother potlucks. This project is both the result and a component of a discursive process engaged in by my respondents and myself; to lin-guistically remove myself from the writing of it would be inaccurate and inappropriate.

My sample of thirty women includes twelve who were or had been in relationships in which children had been conceived within the lesbian relationship. Another fifteen women were or had been in relationships in which children had been conceived in prior heterosexual relationships. One woman in the sample was counted as a member of each group because she had in the past been in each type of relationship. Including this one overlapping case, my working sample is twenty-seven. A third group was composed of three women who were or had been in relationships in which the reproductive decision-making process had been followed through to the point where it was decided that motherhood would not be pursued. Because this latter group is so small and because its members were not pursuing motherhood, it is excluded from this analysis. For the sake of simplicity I refer to the two groups of twelve and fifteen women as Groups A and B respectively.

Of the twelve Group A women I was able to interview both members of five couples. One woman was single and one woman, whose partner declined to be interviewed, was in a very long-term relationship. Because this woman was in a relationship and she and her partner had raised their children together from conception to adulthood, I include this pair when I speak of *six* Group A couples. The length of relationships among Group A couples (at the time of interviewing) ranged from three and a half to twenty-eight years.

Group B was composed of six couples whose relationships ranged from seven months to seven years in duration. This group also included three single women (one of whom, as mentioned above, is also counted in Group A).

Since I was engaged in qualitative research, I gathered relatively little information that was purely quantitative. Nonetheless, I did request a few demographic details of the respondents, which can be used to characterize the sample. The decision to couch this discussion in general terms is the result of a struggle over how to preserve confidentiality while also representing the women who spoke to me. I have rejected the use of demographic-type characteristics to identify individual women in the body of my discussion. The lesbian community tends to be insular and interconnected. The community of lesbian women having children by donor insemination is relatively small. Thus if I were to introduce a quote by attributing it to, say, 'Lynn, a thirty-seven-year-old, professional mother of an infant girl,' it would probably be readily apparent to at least some readers to whom I was referring. Since this was a concern expressed by several of the participants I have chosen to avoid this technique completely.

Nonetheless, it is necessary that we have some sense of who these women are and some of the details of their lives. The sample divided itself into the two groups, and when we consider demographic features of these groups we see some important similarities and differences. We must remember, of course, that because the sample was gathered by the snowball method, it cannot be considered random or, statistically speaking, representative. In particular, it is estimated (by sample members and myself) that a significant proportion of the lesbian population have children who were conceived in previous heterosexual relationships. It is impossible to know the exact number, but I am confident that my sample of fifteen constitutes a very small segment of this population in Alberta.

The sample of twelve women who were involved in donor insemination appeared to constitute a sizeable proportion of the Albertan lesbian population who had already had children by this means. This population appears to be expanding rapidly, however, and it is impossible to know how many women are engaged in the process of being inseminated. Thus, again, we can assume only that this sample constitutes a portion of the total population of lesbian women who are pursuing or who have used donor insemination in Alberta. A sample, however, does not need to be representative to provide evidence of common issues, concerns, and experiences or to generate hypotheses through exploration.

Before I discuss the characteristics of the individual groups, I want to explore an aspect of the overall sample that I was originally made aware of by the difficulty I experienced in initiating contact with sample members. This difficulty indicated several things to me. First, the lesbian community is extremely protective and very suspicious of anyone doing research on them (even a sister member of the community). Second, various factions of the community may have no knowledge of each other or have poor contact with each other. For example, those women who visit the bars may not personally know any lesbian mothers whom they could contact and tell about my ads. This, in turn, indicates that, third, lesbian mothers may have relatively few social contacts or engage in few activities with people outside their families and circles of friends.

These suppositions were confirmed by several of the women who spoke of feeling isolated. There are numerous dimensions to this isolation. The mothers of babies and young children, especially those who stayed home with the children, felt isolated from the world at large. They empathized with the common sentiment of stay-at-home mothers of young children, in the sense of feeling isolated and separated from each other in their individual homes and spending the day only in the company of children.[4]

Many felt unable to alleviate this situation, however, by seeking the company of other young mothers. They felt alienated from these other women because they are *lesbian* mothers. One respondent, Kim, spoke of another young mother on her block whom she often saw when they were both out with the babies. On the day I interviewed Kim, this other mother had stopped Kim on the street and struck up a conversation. She had suggested that the two of them get together for tea soon. Kim had been noncommittal in her response. She explained to me that although she would enjoy having someone to 'do tea' with, she felt that if she pursued a friendship with this woman then sooner or later she would have to 'come out' to her. This would require a tremendous amount of emotional energy on Kim's part and, based on Kim's experiences, the woman's discomfort with that information would probably spell the end of the friendship. Thus Kim could not see the point of making the effort to establish the friendship in the first place.

Conversely, many of the mothers also felt unable to turn to the lesbian community for any kind of broad social support. There are two main components to the feeling of alienation here. The first is attitudinal. Several of the women felt rejected by the lesbian community. They felt that some members of the lesbian community were uncomfortable and somewhat suspicious of motherhood, as if 'real' lesbians would never pursue motherhood.[5] The other dimension is situational. Many women said that the demands and constraints of motherhood simply did not allow them to have very elaborate social lives. This, of course, is quite common for any couple or single parent with young children.

What emerges is a picture of a population of mothers who sometimes have relatively little contact with the general lesbian community, who have fairly small, tight social groups around them, and who have proba-

---

4 See, for example, Oakley (1974, 1976) and Luxton et al. (1990) for discussions of the isolation and loneliness associated with being a homemaker.
5 Day (1990) discusses the discomfort some members of the lesbian community have with the idea of lesbian parenting. This rejection is sometimes based on the notion that lesbian mothers are emulating the heterosexual model and are thus not being true to their lesbian identity. There is also often a belief that 'real' lesbians simply would have no interest in becoming mothers (perceived to be a heterosexual desire).

Table 1
Demographic characteristics of overall sample

	Group A Child(ren) conceived within lesbian relationship	Group B Child(ren) from previous heterosexual relationship
Total number (women)	12	15
Age range (women)	28–46	26–42
Mean age	34.5	35.0
Education levels	High school: 3 Some post-secondary: 7 Undergraduate degree: 2	High school: 1 Some post-secondary: 5 Undergraduate degree: 6 Graduate or professional degree: 3
Range of duration of relationship	3.5–28 yrs.	7 mos. – 7 yrs.
Mean annual income (couples)	$39,000	$47,000
Total number of children	8	22
Age range (children)	8 mos. – 19 yrs.	7 yrs. – 22 yrs.

Table 2
Method of impregnation and child's awareness of this method (Group A)

	Donor insemination		Sexual intercourse		
Will child(ren) have access to donor information?	Known donor	Unknown donor	Informed donor	Uninformed donor	Totals
Yes	1	3	1	0	5
No	0	0	0	1	1
Totals	1	3	1	1	6

bly sought each other's acquaintance by necessity. This would explain why the community was difficult to gain access to in the first place, but once entered was very amenable to the snowball method of sampling.

As mentioned previously, the sample breaks into two groups: Group A (children conceived within lesbian relationships) and Group B (children conceived within prior heterosexual relationships). Some of the characteristics of groups A and B are summarized in tables 1 and 2.

As shown in table 1, the mean age of women in Groups A and B was 34.5 and 35 respectively. The age range of the two groups was also very similar, with Group A ranging from twenty-eight to forty-six years and Group B ranging from twenty-six to forty-two years. It is striking, therefore, that the six couples and three single women in Group B had a total of twenty-two children of whom fourteen were at least fourteen years old, whereas the six couples and one individual in Group A had a total of only eight children of whom only two were older than four years.

Each group had a high level of education. Seventy-five per cent of Group A, for example, had at least some post-secondary education while 17 per cent held an undergraduate degree. Ninety-three per cent of Group B had at least some post-secondary education, with 60 per cent holding at least an undergraduate degree. Perhaps in keeping with the differences in education levels, the mean income also differed between the two groups. The mean annual income of Group A couples was $39,000, while the same figure for Group B couples was $47,000.

It is important to note here that all members of both sample groups were white and, as we can see, predominantly middle class. The homogeneity of the sample is probably due in part to the sample-generating method since women were referring me to their friends and acquaintances. Although single and partnered lesbian mothers exist in all demographic groups, I think it is possible, in the case of the donor-insemination families, that of all demographic groups, these are the women who are most likely to have (or feel that they have) the financial and material resources to pursue motherhood with another woman.

Another area of apparent homogeneity in the sample was the common identification by all respondents of themselves as feminist. Since there is a wide variety to feminist beliefs, a question I did not pursue in depth with individual respondents, knowing they all identified themselves as feminist does not necessarily tell us anything about their individual beliefs. All participants did believe, however, that their feminist beliefs informed their approaches to mothering, as we will see in their discussions in following chapters. We must be careful not to take this common identification as a sign that all lesbians are also feminists. People tend to choose as friends and acquaintances others who share similar beliefs and it is thus not surprising that a sample gathered by the snowball method would manifest this commonality.

Women of other ethnic origins, social classes, and ideologies were not purposely excluded – I was simply not referred to them. We should bear in mind, however, that ethnic, class, and ideological differences can be meaningful when we are considering women's experiences of mother-hood. The limitations in this sample indicate the need for further research in other communities, with women from all social strata and all ethnic groups, if we hope to gain a comprehensive picture of lesbian mothering in Canada.

Table 2 summarizes the specific decisions Group A women made in terms of how to achieve pregnancy. Four of the six couples chose donor insemination. Three of these couples were able to use anonymous donors procured through an informal network of lesbian mothers. One couple chose to have known donors. All four couples are willing to let their children have information about the donors, although they differ regarding the age they feel would be most appropriate for the children to be so informed.

Two of the couples achieved pregnancy through sexual intercourse. This does not make these women equivalent to Group B women, who became pregnant while in heterosexual relationships. Neither of these women had an actual romantic relationship with the man involved, although each knew the man, cared about him, and chose him for this reason. They had intercourse specifically for the purpose of getting pregnant. Because of this they consider the process equivalent to self-insemination and the men equivalent to donors; intercourse was merely the most readily available means for them to transport the sperm from point A to point B. One woman informed the donor of her intentions and the other did not. These methods of achieving pregnancy and the experiences associated with them will be taken up in greater detail in chapter 3.

Based on these demographic-type details and other information obtained during the interviews, it is possible to draw a profile of a 'typical' member of each group. Such a distillation of information puts us at a certain distance from the individual respondents, which is un-fortunate. But since each woman cannot be presented individually, these profiles can provide useful summaries of some of the life details of the members of the two groups. We must remember, of course, that the profiles are composites that do not describe individual women.

The typical Group A woman left her parents' house in her late teens or early twenties. She may have already identified herself as a lesbian or she began to do so by her early twenties. She spent her twenties working and upgrading her education with a year or two of further training. She had very little support from her parents during these years. She may have been in two or three relationships during her twenties. In her late twenties or early thirties she met her current partner. She may have come out to her family and friends at that time.

She and her partner probably started discussing their desire to have one or more children very early in the relationship. After waiting a year or two to test the stability of the relationship, they started exploring the means of achieving pregnancy. Once they decided how to get pregnant and made the arrangements, it generally took less than six months of insemination to achieve pregnancy. If a woman had not already done so, she came out to her family sometime during the pregnancy.

The parents and siblings of the biological mother were typically dismayed initially but then came around and became rather excited about the grandchild, niece, or nephew. The parents of the non-biological mother may or may not have accepted the baby, but they almost certainly did not acknowledge it as their grandchild or respect it as their daughter's child. The non-biological mother's siblings tended to be more accepting than her parents.

Once the child was born, the typical Group A couple tried to arrange for at least one partner to stay home with the baby. Sometimes this role alternated, with the partners working opposing part-time shifts or seasonal jobs. There was general reluctance to put the child into child care much before age two, although this could create economic hardships for the family. The lesbian community (especially close friends) provided vital emotional and material support that in many ways compensated for the lack of support from the couple's families of origin.

The typical Group B woman married quite young (by her early twenties), at which time she probably discontinued any education or employment in which she might have been engaged. She soon had two or three children in close succession. She was separated or divorced by her late twenties, at which time she probably went back to school (generally to finish her undergraduate degree or to pursue graduate or professional training) or returned to work.

She came out as a lesbian in her late twenties or early thirties and had been involved in one or two lesbian relationships at the time of the interview. At that time she was completing her education or embarking on a professional career. At the time of the research she was also involved in what she considered her first (and, she hoped, only) serious lesbian relationship.

She probably had sole custody of her children. Her partner might also have custody of one or more children. The five women who did not have children were similar to the typical Group A woman in so far as they had identified themselves as lesbian most of their adult lives and had never been involved in a heterosexual relationship. The couple created a blended family wherein they deal with many of the standard step-parenting issues as well as issues centring on their lesbianism as it affects their children, kin networks, and social circles.

There is a significant point about these profiles that must be noted. The Group B profile captures a set of women at a particular point in the life cycle. This is probably a result of the sample-generating method inasmuch as friends tend to be approximately the same age and hold similar family statuses. Since this sample captures a point in time, a point in a process, it could have included women five years younger or ten years older. Their stories would likely have been similar. They would simply have been caught at different points in the life cycle.

The women in Group A are not for the most part a portion of a larger group of women captured at a certain point in time. A sample of women five years younger or ten years older could probably not have been found. Self-insemination (S.I.) and donor insemination (D.I.) by a meaningful number of lesbian women are occurring now for the first time, and it is those women in their late twenties to mid-thirties who are pursuing motherhood by these means.[6] Such techniques are growing in popularity today among a particular group of women, and there is no reason to believe that this trend will reverse in the near future.

With the matter of research design behind us, we can now turn to some of the issues and themes that emerged from the research. The next chapter explores the concept and experience(s) of the *desire* to mother and the awareness of choice. It also explores the content of reproductive decision-making. In chapter 3 I consider the route to motherhood followed by the D.I. couples. Chapter 4 explains the process by which the Group B women became lesbian mothers. Chapter 5 investigates the nature of mothering and motherhood, and chapter 6 discusses some of the issues and characteristics that are most relevant to life within a lesbian family.

---

6 'Donor insemination' is a general term that denotes insemination using donor sperm, regardless of who performs the insemination. 'Self-insemination,' as I use the term, is donor insemination that one performs on oneself or on one's partner.

2

Reproductive Decision-Making

For the first time in human history, reproductive planning with a relatively high degree of success is possible. Those of us who grew to adulthood as the idea of reproductive choice was being elaborated are in a very real sense the first generation of 'choosers.' We are the first ones who were affected in childhood by the planning ideology, and who must now put that ideology to work in our adult lives.

The use of contraceptives, at least until the last twenty years or so, has been guided by the various reasons *not* to have children at any given point in time. Pro-choice advocates have always demanded that women be able to exercise contraceptive control in the sense of not bearing children they do not want, whatever the reasons. But the pro-choice movement, which prompted the widespread availability of contraception, has evolved into an ideology of reproductive freedom that extends beyond the right to decide *not* to get pregnant or give birth. The availability of contraception, which allows people to consciously decide when and why they do not want to have children, also requires people to consciously decide when and why they *do* want to have children.[1]

1 This is not to suggest that people have not always tried to exercise reproductive control. The use of contraceptives dates back to ancient times. See, for example, McLaren and McLaren (1986) for a discussion of contraceptive history in Canada. My argument, however, is that these tactics were developed and utilized out of a desire to limit or avoid pregnancy. The most salient motivating factor was the desire not to parent, or not to parent another child, or not to parent another child at a particular time or under particular circumstances.

This kind of reproductive control is a precursor and component of an ideology of choice, an ideology that is partly based on the expectation that contemporary women are not merely identifying the times and conditions under which they wish to avoid pregnancy. Women today are expected to *plan* their 'reproductive careers,' a central compo-

But how do we decide? How do we know how to decide? What criteria do we use in making our decision? We have created the necessity to decide, but we have yet to create the underlying decision-making process. This process is almost arbitrary in that each woman must search through the details of her own life to find guidelines that will enable her to make an informed decision.

Women in exclusively lesbian relationships do not have to make any effort to avoid pregnancy and thus do not have to worry about when and why they do not want children. But they do have to figure out if, why, and when they do want children. These two decisions are two sides of the same coin, but it is only recently that the ideology of choice, accompanied by medical and technological advancements, has expanded from the choice not to have a baby to include the choice to pursue pregnancy, even under conditions that previously would have been considered difficult or prohibitive.[2] Because lesbian women in lesbian relationships must deal only with the latter side of the choice issue, and must do so consciously, knowingly manipulating their options, they can give us some insight into the process whereby all women come to decide that they will pursue motherhood.

CHOICE AS VALUE

Sometime around the third grade, my peers and I began to question whether we had been 'planned' or were 'accidents.' We trooped solemnly home to grill our mothers on this unsettling question, and reported back to our friends in the school yard the answers we had received. I forget now what those answers were, but I do remember that most of us emerged from the inquiry reassured. We had been wanted; we were not accidental.

---

nent of which is deciding *when* and *why* to have children. It is assumed that women (and men) actively *choose* if and when to have children, even though the criteria for making such a decision can be, at best, murky; and even though varying socio-economic statuses, ethnicities, places of residence (e.g., rural or urban), and religious or cultural constraints mean that not all women (or men) have equal access either to contraception or to reproductive assistance (e.g., sperm banks and in-vitro fertilization).

2 Conditions such as sterility previously had to be either simply accepted or 'resolved' by such alternatives as adoption. Today, the fact that fewer 'desirable' babies/children are available for adoption, combined with growing pro-natalist sentiment, has motivated many people to attempt to achieve pregnancy despite physiological or social obstacles.

Not until many years later did I realize that my peers and I, having been conceived in the early 1960s, had probably not been 'planned' as we would use that word today. Although our parents may have had access to some form of contraception, and although some pregnancies were certainly experienced as accidental or planned, the concept of reproductive choice had not itself been meaningfully elaborated. By the early 1970s, however, the idea of choice had become highly meaningful to my friends and me. By some means, and I have no recollection how, the concept of choice had, in the passage from one moment of childhood to another, permeated our consciousnesses. And we understood very well what it meant: the 'planned child' was the wanted child, while the 'accident' was the child who had not been desired beforehand, had not been actively striven for, but had been kept nonetheless as a card dealt by fate.

Is the outcome of the reproductive choices we make less important today than the fact that we have made the choices? We are now in a position to decide whether we want to have babies or not, a decision that we have never had to make in this way before. In the minds of my third-grade peers, the planning, the *choice*, was the *proof* of the desire. This logic still informs at least some of us. As Kim, a D.I. mother, recounted:

I have a friend who had a baby, wasn't married, you know, screwed around. Now her kid's seven, and she doesn't know what to do. And I say, 'well, tell him you used insemination.' ... She thinks that's a more positive thing ... She feels ashamed of what she did, and so if she'd rather tell the kid that she was inseminated, then the kid feels wanted and loved and not that the kid wrecked [her] life. I think that's important, that kids need to feel that.

Kim believed that her own child, Lucy, would have an emotional advantage over other children who knew they had fathers but whose fathers were absent:

In a lot of ways it will be so much nicer for her to know that she was chosen, like we chose to have her and we really want her. And a lot of kids are saying, 'I don't have a father 'cause he doesn't love me and he doesn't love my mommy,' and, you know, I think ... that's a lot of good stuff for Lucy, and it's a positive thing for her.

Denise, another D.I. mother, echoed this sentiment:

[I] really resent anybody who just goes out and makes a baby. I think they short-change themselves and all involved, and especially the child, because I suggest that half the problems with the things that are happening in the world today is because there is a whole bunch of children who weren't wanted, and it wasn't a decision ... I think we have to get back to having them because they're what we want and need and respect in our lives.

Denise talked about returning to the values of a time when babies were conceived because they were wanted as well as needed. But what time was that? In pre-industrial societies, for example, children were often needed to support the family economy. What does it mean, however, to *want* them? Is 'wanting' relevant in the absence of choice or control?

Of course, today we do have choice and control, and it is our desires, the *wanting*, that must guide us in the choices we make. Making reproductive choices is no easy task. Each of us must grapple with what it means to choose whether or not to have a child, and we must be able to justify our choices to ourselves and often to others. Every course of reproductive action is a choice (even if our choice is to leave reproduction to fate), and we are held accountable for the choices we make.

How then do we navigate the course we have chosen for ourselves? I believe there are at least three distinct tasks that exercising reproductive choice requires of us: deciding *whether* we want to have children, figuring out *why* we do want them and why we do not, and deciding *when* to have them. For lesbian women, single women, and women who have trouble conceiving, a fourth question that must be answered is *how* pregnancy will be achieved. Answering these questions constitutes our reproductive decision-making process.

CONSIDERING MOTHERHOOD

Surprisingly little research has been done on the actual process of reproductive decision-making. The studies that have been conducted focus on heterosexual women and couples, and usually investigate what happens when a couple discovers that they have a fertility problem and must make a decision about the parenthood options still available to them (see Crowe 1985; Rowland 1987). The most thorough investigation into reproductive decision-making (under 'normal' circumstances) by heterosexual women was conducted by Currie (1988). The women in Currie's sample spoke of having to weigh various concerns, such as career stability and financial security, against their desire to mother.

Currie's conclusions suggest that these women were not so much decid-ing *whether* to pursue motherhood as deciding *when* to pursue it. But Currie contends that the 'when,' which her respondents spoke of as 'the right time,' was not a matter of *time* at all. Rather it was a particular configuration of material or structural factors, including career and finances, that determined the best time to have a baby.

When asked about their decision-making, the D.I. mothers in my sam-ple described a process of addressing issues and answering questions. Strikingly, the question of whether or not to pursue motherhood was seldom raised. Several of the women explained that they had simply always assumed that they would have children. Similarly, many of the couples revealed that they had known early in their relationship that they would, or at least wanted to, pursue motherhood. So, for many of the women, there was no real decision-making about *whether* to have children; they always knew they would. It was the logistics of reaching this goal that had to be decided. Others argued that it was impossible to make a decision about having children. As Evelyn put it:

Well, it's like getting married. It's like deciding your career. You can't really make a decision on it until after it's happened because every situation is so dif-ferent and every person is so different.

Nancy made a similar point:

You can't worry about all the details, and there's stuff that comes up, but you deal with them as they come. And that, I think, is what we do in our regular lives anyway, really. You just do it.

But lesbian women cannot just 'do' pregnancy. Key decisions must be made at each stage in the decision-making process. What started this process for many women was the discovery that it was possible for them to fulfil their desire to become mothers. 'When we realized that we could do it,' Wendy said, 'then I think the decision-making process started there.' Part of this realization came about when the women found a man or men who were willing to donate sperm. As Wendy explained:

Once this person had said, 'yeah, I'd love to do it,' then all of a sudden it became a reality. And then it was like, 'Yes, let's go ahead and do it.' And that's what we did, you know. It was just a matter of sort of working out the logistics.

Denise offered an overview of the process she and Wendy had followed:

There's definitely a process as a couple that I think, again, that any straight or gay couple goes through, where you ... start off your relationship, you're in love, you think about having a baby because that's part of being in love, and then it goes from there. And then you decide that the relationship is stable enough and that you are staying together, and your lives are stable enough generally that you get down to an almost serious discussion of having a baby. And then you get over the fear of having a baby, and then you get down to actually producing a baby. I mean, it was definitely conscious.

My interviews indicated that while the decision-making process that women go through is not a linear one, there clearly is a point A (recognizing and acknowledging the desire to mother) and a point B (attempting to become mothers). Between these two points are issues and concerns that must be addressed, questions that must be answered, and decisions that must be made. Frequently, the reasons for having a child must be considered, and the couple must determine the best time to pursue pregnancy. Although these factors overlap in real life, I will consider them separately in order to illuminate some of the major steps in the journey towards motherhood.

ARTICULATING THE DESIRE TO MOTHER

One assumption guiding my research was that lesbian women who pursue D.I. pregnancies must at some point experience the desire to have a child, and must be able to identify that desire. All the respondents were able to describe what it meant to desire a child and, frequently, what that desire felt like. Although the women differed in their experience of the desire, some common themes emerged.

Several women said that they had always wanted children and had grown up assuming they would have them (that is, until they were confronted with the logistical requirements of achieving pregnancy while in a lesbian relationship). As Rose explained:

As kids in our – in my – generation, we'd been nurtured to grow up and become mothers, and I guess that was really instilled in me at a young age, and I really accepted that and I really felt comfortable with that ... I think that that idea is put into your head at a really young age – 'this is what I *must* do,' not that that was the must, but I think that sort of, when I could enhance my relationship, then that's what I wanted to do.

Many women claimed that there is a biological aspect to the desire to mother, ranging from feeling one's 'biological clock' to a complete 'physical yearning.' Some of the women who expressed this idea did so with a guilty acknowledgment of its contentiousness among feminists. But to these same women it made sense that there might be a biological aspect to the desire to have a child, since impregnation, gestation, parturition, and lactation are fundamentally physiological processes. Elly addressed the relationship between biology and socialization:

The way I got pregnant and how it happened with me just seems to make me feel like there is something in my body. Now, who knows, that might be internalized socialization. Our socialization affects our bodies. Our minds and bodies are connected.

Elly experienced her desire for pregnancy primarily as a physical yearning, which she described as a desire 'to mate ... to have a little baby grow in me, which isn't nurturing, which is having a child.' She defined 'mating' not as having intercourse or being pregnant, but rather as

physically having a sperm and ovum join in your womb and having it implant and growing that little creature. And that's quite different from the nurturing. I would say that I'm sure the nurturing is socialized into us.

At another point in our interview, Elly explained:

I just wanted to be pregnant. I felt ripe. It's weird, but my body just felt like it wanted to get pregnant. And I just wanted to, I really wanted to have a baby and have a child, and I had realized that. I guess I had just been struck over and over ... that I wanted children in my life, and that would be one of the most worthwhile things I could do in my life, or that would be one of the most enriching things I could do in my life.

Kim related a similar experience:

I think it's almost a physical yearning at times. It's a desire to carry on, to have someone when you get older, you know. Like maybe have grandchildren.

Several interviewees mentioned non-biological aspects of the desire to have children. Some explained that they love and enjoy children and thus wanted one or more of their own. Some women said they wanted the opportunity to do a better job of raising children than their parents had done. Noreen said:

I think it was the opportunity to parent, to make it different, 'cause there was a lot of things about my parenting that, which is typical, that I didn't feel my parents did as good a job parenting as I would have done or I would do. And I still feel that, you know, that I do a better job.

Iris was among those women who voiced a desire to produce and raise a child who would become an outstanding human being:

There's an attraction of wanting to raise a child who could make a difference in the world, who could learn from everything I've done, who could learn from having mothers who are, you know, slightly left, and the challenge of wanting to raise a child to be things that we couldn't have had. You know, I want Steven [son] to know what racism is. I want Steven to know what sexism is. I want him to understand that. I want him to know that it's not right. And, you know, when we were kids we were subliminally induced with all of that. There's a desire for that. You can't do that with a dog. You can't make your dog non-racist. I don't think it's really much more than that. It's a desire to give your love to another friend, another being, another person, um, to have an intimate relationship with another person, to share our success of living.

Another reason the respondents gave for wanting a child was curiosity – to know what it is like to raise a child and not miss out on this experience. Some women spoke of the sense of completion that motherhood can bring. As Blaire described it:

I guess really simply, um, I suppose it makes me feel full. You know I have a desire to be a mother and that if I denied it, you know, I would not be completely whole. So to want to be a mother, I suppose, tells me that this is Blaire. It feels to me that that's Blaire. That's the Blaire I know and the Blaire I feel, and in a way it keeps me very much on the ground. It's hard to explain what it means to want to be a mother in any other way than I guess it's part of who I am. It's not all of me, but it's an important part, important that denying it I really would not be as content as I am.

Another benefit of motherhood sought by some of the women was the self-confrontation it requires. Again, Blaire explained:

Probably this is the whole conscious process that lesbians go through in wanting to have kids, or me anyway. I have to not live through him. I have to not make him do what I think he should be doing. I have to learn to know him. I have to listen to him and practise understanding him so it makes me face my ideas, my assumptions, my gut reactions of my deep-down notions of motherhood and things like that, and caring and respect for other people no matter what age they are. So it does make me face myself, and I guess that's important for me and that's probably part of why I want to be a mother too.

Several women saw motherhood as an enriching experience and desired it for this reason. Some believed that having a child would enhance a relationship that had evolved to the point where it *could* be enhanced by the addition of a child. I will address this idea more fully in my discussion of 'the right time.'

A few women spoke of the desire becoming a *need*, particularly in the face of obstacles to the fulfilment of the desire. At the time Noreen wanted to conceive, there was no D.I. available and she knew no men with whom she was willing to have intercourse for this purpose:

I was starting to feel like if I can't be inseminated, and I can't do it physically, then I'm not going to have a baby – and that turned it more to a desperate need. You know, like I'm getting desperate: 'how am I going to do this?' And then it became irrational, like it was almost like a driven force, like I was going to do it any way I could. It was very obsessive actually, I think.

Denise said she never really intended to have children until her doctor told her she probably could not:

Even though I loved [babies], I was never going to have one, never be a part of that. And then when the doctor told me, at age twenty-three, [that] my chances were very slim, at best, to have one, I went, 'Hold on, that's not fair; other women can have them and now I can't.' So I, all of a sudden it started kicking in more. I was like, well, you know, 'It's my right to have them. You can't tell me I can't have them.' So then I batted that around.

I asked the women if, in their desire to have a child, they wanted to experience pregnancy and birth, or raising a child, or both. For many, these two components of mothering were so linked that they had never considered them separately. Many answered that they had been striving for the whole experience. This was true even for the non-biological D.I. mothers, who frequently spoke of insemination, pregnancy, and birth as an experience that they shared with their partners (e.g., 'When *we* were pregnant ... '). Only when the achievement of pregnancy was frustrated did the two components of mothering become conceptually separated. Kim, for example, had had considerable difficulty bringing a pregnancy to term. In answer to my question about which element of motherhood she had been seeking, she said:

I wanted both, but more I wanted to raise a child. I think I realized that at the end when I started to think I might have to consider other options ... like adoption or whatever. It would have been upsetting but not devastating. I really enjoy watching children grow and that kind of thing. I guess I feel privileged that I was able to give birth.

A few women said they wanted to raise a child but had no pressing desire to personally go through the pregnancy and birth. This was never a problem because these women had partners who did want the experience of pregnancy and birth. Only Tina said that she had never seriously considered motherhood until her partner brought up the idea:

I think that was because I hadn't thought of that as an option so, you know, if you don't see it as an option it's not really something that you pursue in any lines of thinking. So I thought, 'Lesbian – no kids, that's it.' So, no, I had never really felt any desire to parent.

When I asked those women who had had children in previous heterosexual relationships about their desire to have children, there was a striking difference in the responses. It is not that these women had not wanted children, but rather that the desire had been felt in a different way. For some, it appears that the decision to get married was tantamount to choosing to have children; children were a 'given' and, as such, did not necessarily have to be carefully planned or actively desired. Having children was part of the life course many of these women assumed they would follow. Many desired children, but that desire was often experienced less poignantly than it was by the women who faced obstacles in achieving pregnancy.

What became clear in the course of the interviews was that the desire to mother was salient to most of these women – and particularly so to the D.I. mothers – even though the nature of the desire varied. It also became evident that *what* was desired and *how* the desire was experienced are inextricably linked. Recognizing and acknowledging the desire to mother, however, is frequently only a small component of the process through which women arrive at motherhood.

PRELIMINARY CONCERNS

Once a couple acknowledged that they wanted to pursue motherhood, they found themselves faced with a number of questions. These ranged from working out the logistics of getting pregnant to reconsidering ideas about parenting and dealing with issues specific to lesbian parents. Sometimes the first question to be settled was which member of the couple was going to have the baby. None of the couples found this a markedly difficult decision to make. Usually one of the partners wanted to get pregnant more than the other one did. Several of the couples decided that the person who most wanted to get pregnant would do so first and then her partner would have the next child. At the time of the interviews, two of the couples were discussing the time when the second pregnancy would be attempted and one couple had decided they probably would not try to have another child.

Often the next question was how pregnancy would be accomplished. As stated in chapter 1, four of the six couples chose to use sperm donors. The other two couples chose to have sexual intercourse with men. I will discuss the women's experiences with these decisions more fully in the next chapter.

Several women explained that they needed to know that their relationship was stable, that it would last. This was an important consideration in defining 'the right time' to pursue pregnancy. The women needed to feel that both partners were committed not only to the relationship, but also to the child and that each truly desired it.

Several women spoke of wanting to explore and re-examine their ideas of motherhood. Many rejected the idea of motherhood that their mothers had embodied; the traditional housewife–mother who attended to everyone's emotional and physical needs and maintained sole responsibility for the domestic realm. This led to discussions about what it would mean to have two mothers and how that would manifest itself in the division of emotional, parenting, and domestic labour. There were also concerns about problems or issues the non-biological mother might face, such as securing her legal status as mother.

Most of the women also had to deal with 'coming out.' Several women waited until they or their partners were pregnant before coming out to their families about their lesbianism. Others who were already 'out' to family, friends, and co-workers felt that pregnancy and parenting required them to be even farther out. Discretion and half-answers to people's questions about their relationship to each other and to the child would no longer do. Many women felt very strongly that their children should not feel shame or trepidation about revealing the 'situation' at home to others. Having a child put these women in contact with the public world in a way they had previously been able to avoid. Even the women who considered themselves completely out sometimes had to brace themselves for the public scrutiny they would be required to face in the future. Many women also said that coming out became a problem for their families, who were now forced to explain how this grandchild, niece, or nephew came into being.

A major concern for all the couples was that one of them, or both of them alternately, be able to stay home with the baby. None was willing to consider day care at that stage in the child's life.

I have offered here only a brief overview of some of the major issues that women faced early on in their pursuit of motherhood because, as I shall point out in subsequent chapters, it was during pregnancy, birth, and parenting that many of these issues were faced and resolved.

RIGHT AND WRONG REASONS FOR PURSUING MOTHERHOOD

It is unlikely that before the era of reproductive choice women discussed the reasons they and other women had children. If you have no choice, you need no reason. And even if you have a choice, if you have grown up in a culture pervaded by the belief that women will and should have children, it is rarely necessary to articulate the reasons for doing so. But today the situation is different. Almost every woman I spoke with mentioned that there are right, or acceptable, reasons for having a baby and wrong, or unacceptable, reasons for doing so. While there was little agreement among the respondents about what qualified as good and bad reasons, the concept of justifying having a baby was meaningful to each.

Many women agreed that babies should not be had for 'selfish' reasons such as having someone who would look after you in later years, having someone who would 'complete' you, having someone who would look like you, or having someone who would live on after you (and thus 'continue' you). What for some women were clearly selfish reasons, however, were for others perfectly acceptable ones. For example, Christine, who had been adopted and had never known anyone with whom she had a biological link, was very sympathetic to the notion of a woman having a child so that she would have someone who looked like her and who was genetically related to her.

The right reasons for having a child were characterized as 'selfless.' The general feeling was one should have a baby not for one's own sake but for the sake of the baby. A woman should decide to have a baby because she wants to nurture it, love it, and help it grow into a well-adjusted adulthood. For D.I. mothers this reasoning also applied to sperm donors. These women hoped that the men were donating sperm for the right (i.e., unselfish) reasons, that they would be sympathetic and compassionate enough to truly want to help them have babies, but not so emotionally involved that they would later assert paternity. One of the D.I. mothers, Iris, believed that 'men who donate sperm to lesbian couples anonymously, and [who] are very quick to say they want no responsibility, do it for the right reasons because they are giving women the freedom to have their own children.'

Although many women were able to articulate what they believed were the right and wrong reasons to have a child (or donate sperm), their discussion of these reasons tended to remain abstract. Many women brought up the subject of reasons spontaneously, yet when I asked if they had identified or analysed those reasons, some of them shifted the conversation to a discussion of the desire to mother. Those who did continue the discussion of reasons tended to say that they had examined their motives to assure themselves that they were not having a child for the wrong reasons. As Kim explained:

[I] thought more about the negative things like 'Is there any reason why I shouldn't?' instead of 'Is there a reason why I should?' 'Cause I feel like I have the right. I can do it, it doesn't matter. And I'd be a better parent than a lot of people, and I might not be as good a parent as a lot of people, but just because I'm a lesbian doesn't mean I shouldn't have babies.

The conviction that choosing to have a baby is a woman's *right*, and the defensiveness about one's ability or right (or both) to mother, were common elements in the interviews, especially when justifications were discussed. The defensiveness is hardly surprising when we consider that all these women have at some point been required to justify their motives or desires to family members and friends. Many of the women reported that when they informed at least some of their immediate family members of their pregnancy, of their attempts to get pregnant, or of their decision to try to get pregnant, the first question they were asked was 'Why?' Heterosexual couples, they believed, would not receive this kind of response from their families. As they see it, people assume that it is natural for a heterosexual couple to want or have a child, but somehow bizarre for lesbians to want the same thing. According to 'common sense,' lesbian women, because of their sexuality, are fundamentally different from heterosexual women, and possibly not even quite whole or natural women.

Lesbian women seeking motherhood also have to face the misconception that there is a link between homosexuality and paedophilia. (People tend to make insinuations about this stereotype rather than directly accuse lesbian family members, friends, or – even more likely – acquaintances). Another common question was 'Why would you want to bring children into *that*?' In the mind of the questioner, 'that' refers to a household whose value system is completely at odds with that of the mainstream society, and wherein the children will be, at best, tainted and, at worst, raised to be homosexual themselves.

The need for lesbian women to justify their motives and defend themselves against such challenges may contribute to the defence of the *right* to reproduce expressed by many of them. The idea that reproductive choice includes both the choice to avoid pregnancy and the choice to pursue pregnancy is not, of course, unique to the lesbian population. It is only one example of how the ideology of reproductive choice manifests itself. It is significant, however, that many lesbian women feel required to incorporate the idea of the right to have children into their defense of their choice to pursue pregnancy.

That the discussion of right and wrong reasons to have children frequently evolved, in the interviews, into a discussion about the desire to mother indicates that these two classes of reasons are closely linked and yet distinct. In other words, the reasons to *have* a child were not the same as the reasons to *want* a child. The former reasons tend to be articulated in more rational terms than the latter. Related to the desire to mother, yet also distinct from it, was the feeling that it was the *right time* to have a baby. This feeling, like the desire to mother, seemed to be most salient among the D.I. mothers as they engaged in their decision-making.

'THE RIGHT TIME'

In the course of researching reproductive decision-making among heterosexual women, Currie (1988: 241–9) found that identifying 'the right time' to have a child was important to many of the women with whom she spoke. When she pressed them to explain what constituted the right time, their answers convinced her that it was not a matter of 'time' at all. Among the factors her respondents mentioned were job security, financial stability, and the ability of partners to be supportive and involved. Currie interpreted these factors as material or structural features of women's lives – external factors that the women had internalized to the point that they were experienced as an internal readiness to mother.

My curiosity having been piqued by this aspect of Currie's work, I endeavoured to determine if 'the right time' was also an important consideration for my lesbian respondents. Many brought up the idea themselves while discussing their desire to mother or to reach a decision. With other women I brought up the subject, asking if they had a sense that it was the right time and what it meant to them. The idea was indeed significant for each of the D.I. mothers with whom I spoke.

Applying Currie's typology of 'internal' and 'material' factors, I found that most of the women's responses contained examples of each. Only a couple of women had what they considered absorbing occupational careers and were looking for a natural break in their careers that would allow them to leave for a while. As Wendy explained:

I guess it was something that, at the point in my life, I was ready to experience ... I had reached a point in my career where I had achieved what I wanted to achieve. And sure, there's always more to achieve, and I'll probably go off in different directions now. But I had done what I had wanted to do, and if I don't ever do anything more, in that field anyway, I'll be happy. I'll be very happy, actually. So I was ready to go on to new things.

It was far more common, however, for the women to have less interesting careers, careers they were ready to leave anyway, or careers they could temporarily leave with no negative repercussions. The struggle that Currie's sample had with balancing the desire for a career and the desire for a child was not often experienced by my respondents.

Of greater concern to the women in my sample was the issue of financial stability. Two of the women felt that it was important (although not absolutely necessary) to be able to own their own homes. The majority of women had wrestled with the question of whether they could afford to have a child. Only two of the couples were so financially secure that this was not a real concern for them. The remaining women had reached the conclusion that there is no such thing as the right time financially, and that if people wait until they feel they have enough money they will wait forever. According to Kim:

There's never a good time to have a baby. Never, like you never have enough money. You never have enough time. So then after a while you just think, 'Basically we have what we need, the minimum of what we need,' and you just dive in and do it.

Many of the respondents believed that while it is instructive for women to assess their financial capabilities, this assessment should not be a deciding factor. As Iris explained:

Well, I think the financial question is a worthy question, but it's certainly not the most important question. It's never financially right to have a child, and if you wait for it to be financially right you're going to be sixty-five and retired.

In short, even though careers and financial stability were occasional concerns for these women – concerns that sometimes had to be addressed in their decision-making – they were generally only marginal elements in determining the right time to pursue motherhood. (This option, it should be pointed out, would be less available to working-class women.) The two most common characteristics of the right time were (1) the presence of a stable relationship with a partner one wanted to co-parent with, and (2) a sense of being emotionally ready.

Several of the women mentioned that although they might have wanted a child in the past, they had either been single or had been in relationships they considered too unstable to bring a child into. Once they found a partner they believed would be a good co-parent, and once they developed a stable relationship they believed would last, it quickly became the right time to pursue motherhood. Iris recalled:

When I was younger I knew I'd like to have a child, but the relationships that I was having were less than satisfying, and I knew I couldn't have a child until I had the right partner. And when I started living with Blaire, I knew then, as

I know now, that we're the right couple to have a child, and that's really important to me – to know that we have the longevity to do it.

Of equal importance was a sense of internal readiness or emotional stability. For some women this required coming to terms with dysfunctional parenting experienced in their own childhoods. For others it simply meant feeling emotionally capable of meeting the challenge of loving and nurturing a child. As Wendy described it:

I guess I just sort of felt ready internally, too. I just sort of felt, you know, I'm at peace with myself and who I am. I feel good about who I am, you know, now I want to share with someone else.

For many women the sense of internal readiness was inextricably linked with the emotional stability of both the relationship and the partner.

For some women age was the signal that the time was right to have a child. Wendy explained:

I started to feel like, well, at thirty years old it was getting too late. Because if you leave it much later than that, you know, you have not just the physical thing, I think, but it's a major readjustment for one thing – which it is anyway – but the older you get I'm sure the harder the adjustment is. And it's harder on the child when they get older to have older parents.

Related to the age factor was the feeling expressed by some of the women that they were physically ready. Wendy said, 'Physically I knew my body was ready.' For Elly, physical readiness combined with meeting the right man to inseminate her made it the right time to pursue pregnancy:

We had met and become attracted to each other, and I completely – This might sound like bunk, but I believed that I wanted to make a baby, like I had a very strong biological urge to make a baby and that was part of the attraction because, I mean, I had been looking for a long time. Every man that I sort of met I thought: Well, where does he live? Who does he know? Is he gay? Do you think he's had men lovers? – like trying to judge his HIV possibilities. I mean, I just had my eye out for a long time, and this guy came along, and he seemed perfect, and he was nice. And all of a sudden it's like, 'Holy shit, I need to do this. I really really need to do this.'

Having the opportunity to become pregnant was also important for some of the other women in that it helped to coalesce other elements into the right time. As Kim explained, 'I think basically I've always been ready. Like I always wanted a baby, and just the circumstances that came to be that we could have one was enough.'

For some women, being able to satisfactorily address all their questions and concerns about parenting was a necessary step in reaching the right time. Some were quick to point out that this questioning did not involve issues arising from their lesbianism. As Denise put it:

It's not part of my mind-set to worry about the fact that I'm gay and I want to have a child. So I never even – I didn't consider it. It would be like worrying about the fact that you're black and you want to have a child. It can't be part of your mind; it can't be part of your decision-making.

Other women did feel, however, that there were questions only lesbian mothers would have to ask themselves – questions such as 'What will the child call us?' and 'How can we guarantee the non-biological mother's rights to the child?' Issues not unique to lesbian women but that still had to be considered by some of the respondents included emotional readiness, which for Blaire involved

just rethinking ... my ideas of parenting, ah, what motherhood meant to me, what fatherhood meant to me. And then we'd talk about what those things meant to ourselves.

Her partner, Iris, elaborated:

I knew that we had questions, all the questions like Is it right? Can we do it? Are we strong enough? Will we be good parents? You know, all the questions. And I knew it was time when we had pretty well drummed up all the questions we could think of and could answer them honestly. So for me, when we knew that all the questions had been thought of, then it was time, the time was right.

In the course of the interviews, it became clear that it was not individual factors but rather a particular combination of them that led women to believe that the time was right. Their overall sense was that their lives were better than ever before, and that was what made it the right time. Before she got pregnant, Noreen recalled:

Things were perfect *but* ... And a lot of times I said that everything's perfect *but* I want us to have a baby, we want a baby. So it was always that little 'but' in there.

A more common sentiment than 'everything's perfect *but* ... ' was 'everything's perfect *and* ... ' Everything was perfect, *and* it was time to add a child (because a child could only contribute positively to the relationship), *and* the relationship (along with the women in it) was stable enough to take on the task of raising a child.

As noted earlier, the stories told by the women in Currie's sample led her to conclude that it was a 'configuration of material circumstances' that constituted 'the right time' (which was not a matter of 'time' at all). In contrast, for the women I interviewed, the right time really was a point in time when all the necessary elements coalesced. Why do our findings differ so? Could it be that heterosexual women face a different sort of decision-making process than lesbian women do? There are several answers to this question.

If more of the D.I. mothers whom I interviewed had been deeply immersed in absorbing careers, perhaps this 'external' feature would have held a greater significance for them. Nevertheless, demographic differences between Currie's sample and my sample cannot explain all the variations in the responses. When I asked the Group B mothers in my sample (those who had had children while in heterosexual relationships) about their sense of the right time, their answers were consistent with what they had told me about their desire to mother. Although it may have been important for them and their husbands to achieve financial and material stability before they started having children, it was a given that they *would* have children. Because choosing a husband is, for the most part, tantamount to choosing a co-parent for one's future children as well, being married and 'settled' was often enough to make it the right time for these women to at least consider having children.

It is unlikely that 'the right time to have children' was as meaningful a concept one hundred or even thirty years ago. Certainly, there have always been *wrong times* to get pregnant – for example, when one is fourteen years old and unwed. The desire to avoid the wrong time is part of what fuelled the fight for reproductive self-determination, and it is probably the main reason contraceptives were sought and invented in the first place. By being married, a woman has already escaped one of the most celebrated wrong times for pregnancy. By choosing a mate and potential co-parent, she meets the basic requirements. When she examines her life in search of guidelines to assist her in her decision-making, she tends to find material factors, such as career stability and financial security, around which she can determine the right time for pregnancy. And because she meets the basic requirements – through marriage – these other elements become primary in her decision-making.

Of primary importance to my lesbian sample in determining the right time was relational and emotional stability. It was finding a stable partner one could co-parent with and establishing oneself in a stable relationship that was, according to various criteria, 'perfect.' Is this not what we assume *marriage* (or at least the ideal of marriage) to be? Thus, whereas being married provides the basic requirements that enable heterosexual women to consider other factors, the primary concern of many lesbian couples is to bring their lives into alignment with some of the ideals we associate with marriage.[3] This emphasis relegates other concerns, such as career and financial stability, to a secondary level of importance.

Thus we can see that my findings and Currie's are not so inconsistent with each other after all. Currie's oversight is that she takes marriage for granted and does not notice that her respondents tend to do so as well. What my sample's responses brought to light is all that is subsumed under the concept of marriage. I do not believe there is a fundamental difference between heterosexual and lesbian women in their determinations of the right time to pursue motherhood. It is simply that lesbian women must be more consciously aware of *all* they are seeking and how they will attain it in a way that heterosexual women can usually avoid.

It is Currie's position that the problem women face in their reproductive decision-making is having to reconcile the structural or material features of their lives with their desire for the emotional and experiential aspects of motherhood. I agree that this is a dilemma but would argue that the fundamental *problem* facing all women is the necessity of making a decision *they do not know how* to make, and that material circumstances are merely *problematic* conditions underlying this situation. Research such as mine and Currie's begins to show how women are able to create their own reproductive decision-making process based on those aspects of their lives that they choose to guide them through it. We have seen that while heterosexual and lesbian women focus on different aspects of their lives, their actual concerns and the process they go through seem to be very similar.

We must remember, however, that the women on whom I have based

---

3 This is not to suggest that lesbian couples seek to emulate heterosexual marriages in terms of division of labour, domestic and parenting roles, and so forth. The women in my sample were seeking stability and emotional commitment, two components of a relationship that we tend to associate most strongly with marriage.

my discussion are ones who knew they wanted children and were able to make the decision. We do not know how large a part this desire plays in enabling women to decide to pursue motherhood, but it seems reasonable to speculate that women who know they want children find it easier to determine the right time. Similarly, women who feel the desire less strongly, or who are less able to identify it, may have less incentive to find or create the right time. That the desire is felt most strongly, or is easiest to identify, in the face of obstacles to its fulfilment is suggested by research on infertile heterosexual couples (Crowe 1985; Rowland 1987). Thus the large proportion of Currie's sample who were undecided and taking contraceptive risks (i.e., using contraceptives inconsistently) may represent the norm for a large proportion of the heterosexual population who do not have to consider or question their desire to pursue parenthood to the same extent that others might. The fact that lesbian women do face obstacles in achieving motherhood, and that they must know what they want and *really* want it, may make them better able to articulate the desire and decision-making process that most heterosexuals take for granted.

There are five different means by which the women in my sample became mothers:

1 impregnation while in a lesbian relationship, either through donor insemination or sexual intercourse with a male;
2 being the partner of a woman who was impregnated while in a lesbian relationship;
3 impregnation via sexual intercourse while in a heterosexual relationship (generally a marriage);
4 becoming involved with a woman who had had a child or children while in a previous heterosexual relationship; and
5 becoming involved with a woman who had had a child while in a previous lesbian relationship.

Although only the third of the above routes to motherhood is the conventional one, all the women in my sample were faced with the task of becoming mothers, and all were faced with the challenge of exploring what motherhood can mean under these different circumstances. The first two routes to motherhood are examined in the next chapter. The latter three are explored in chapter 4. Chapter 5 examines the experiences and challenges that mark each of these types of motherhood.

3

Achieving Motherhood: D.I. Families

The traditional means of achieving pregnancy, heterosexual intercourse, is something many lesbian women do not consider a viable option. The choice not to have heterosexual intercourse is frequently a component of a woman's self-identification as a lesbian. Further, it is not uncommon for lesbian women to have relatively few male contacts in their social circles. Thus, even if a woman were willing to have sex with a man, she may not know a man who would be acceptable.

In a sense, then, lesbian women in lesbian relationships are structurally or circumstantially infertile. Canadian infertility clinics often adhere to a policy (explicit or implicit) of helping only married heterosexual couples achieve pregnancy. In June 1992 the Foothills hospital in Calgary announced that it would start making D.I. services available to single and lesbian women. Unfortunately for the women in my sample, this had not been an option at the time they were trying to get pregnant.

Many sperm banks are affiliated with infertility clinics and operate to store sperm of and for their chosen clientele. Thus people denied access to the clinic also are denied access to the affiliated sperm bank, with both its stores of sperm and its technological capacity for sperm storage. An exception to this rule, in Canada, is the Toronto-based company ReproMed, which ships sperm across Canada and does not screen recipients based on sexual orientation or financial status or stability. Because ReproMed is a commercial agency, however, the costs involved in procuring its sperm can be high. Further, ReproMed ships sperm only to qualified medical personnel, eliminating the option of self-insemination.[1]

In Alberta few private physicians are willing to assist lesbian women

---

1 Information package from ReproMed Ltd., Toronto, Canada.

by performing inseminations. In Calgary, in late 1990, a small group of doctors demonstrated their opposition to the Foothills hospital's policy of banning access to single and lesbian women by offering to assist these women (Walker 1990: B1). The biggest deterrent for women wishing to use these doctors' services, apart from regional inaccessibility, is the expense involved. Since Alberta Health Care does not cover insemination, the recipient must pay all medical fees, purchase the sperm, and pay any shipping and storage costs. A Calgary woman inseminated by a doctor who brings in sperm from ReproMed could easily face an initial charge of $1000 followed by a charge of at least $500 per cycle.[2]

All the women in my Group A sample chose self-insemination over any form of medically assisted insemination. Some said they would have used a facility such as the Foothills infertility clinic had it been available to them at the time. Many said they wished that, at minimum, they had been able to obtain information or guidance from the infertility clinic. All of the couples in my sample felt very much alone in their pursuit of pregnancy. For many couples the process of becoming and being pregnant proved to be a bit of an obstacle course, with many challenges to be met and difficulties to be negotiated.

SELF-INSEMINATION

Four of the six Group A couples achieved pregnancy via self-insemination with donor sperm. The most complicated aspect of this low-tech procedure is coordinating all the people who may be involved in getting the sperm from the body of the donor into the body of the recipient. Three of the four couples were aided by a person who helped procure donors and transport the sperm. These procurers/runners belonged to a support group that performed these services to the best of its abilities. Donors and recipients thus remained unknown to each other.

One of these couples was inseminating in the mid-1980s, when information about AIDS and HIV was only beginning to reach the public. Thus it did not occur to either the recipients or the runner to have the prospective donors screened for HIV. By specifying that they wanted donors who had been in long-term monogamous relationships, and by ensuring that medical histories of the donors were taken, the recipients hoped to minimize the risk of sexually transmitted disease.

2 These figures were obtained through personal correspondence with a Calgary physician who offers D.I. services. She requested anonymity.

The other three couples requested that their donors undergo HIV testing. The couple who used known donors simply asked their donors to have the tests done. For the remaining two couples, the runner arranged for the donors to take tests for HIV. A second set of HIV tests was done six months later. Donors were also required to have medical exams (including testing for sexually transmitted diseases) and to complete a medical history, which would be made available to the prospective recipients. If everything else was acceptable, the donors could begin donating after the second negative HIV test.

Donors were asked not to engage in 'risky' behaviour, such as unprotected sex, after their first HIV test. They were asked to inform the runner (or, in the case of known donors, the recipients) if they engaged in such behaviour so that the donors could be withdrawn from the program. We encounter here a disadvantage to using fresh sperm rather than frozen sperm procured through a sperm bank. Sperm banks test the donor at the point of initial donation and then store the sperm for at least six months, during which time repeated HIV tests are performed on the donor. If the donor is HIV-negative six months after the initial donation then that first donation is cleared for use. This allows for the incubation period the HIV may require before it becomes detectable. It is impossible to subject the donors of fresh sperm to these rigorous testing procedures. The practice of checking a potential fresh-sperm donor twice, six months apart, before he is accepted as a donor confirms only that he probably was not infected at the time of the first test. This practice provides no certainty about the donor's safety at the time of the second test, after which he would be donating. Nonetheless, the recipients were willing to take the risk with respect to the truthfulness of the donors and the reliability of the available testing.

The recipients of unknown-donor sperm had meanwhile been instructed to chart their basal temperatures and employ any other means that would give them an accurate understanding of their fertility. When the time came to begin insemination, the recipient was encouraged to use an ovulation-predictor kit for greater accuracy.

Each recipient had two donors who would donate on alternating days. The women chose to have two donors so that they could be inseminated three or four times per cycle without seriously depleting one donor's sperm count. Another perceived advantage to having two donors, for those who had unknown donors, was that even if the recipient somehow discovered the identities of the donors, she would still not know which one was the 'father.' Ideally, the recipient would be inseminated the day before ovulation, the day of ovulation, and the two days following ovulation. For optimum results, the insemination was to be carried out at the same time daily, if possible.

Donors were instructed to ejaculate into sterilized jars or sterile specimen containers and then to put the container in a wool sock before placing it in a paper bag. The anonymous donors handed the sperm over to the runner, who kept the sperm at body temperature in her armpit or inside her coat as she drove it to the recipient's residence or to a prearranged meeting place. The known donors transported the sperm to the recipient's residence themselves.

The recipient or her partner would use a small, needleless syringe to remove the semen from the container and insert it into the recipient's vagina. The recipient remained inclined, with pelvis raised, for at least half an hour. All four couples achieved pregnancy in a maximum of six cycles of insemination, although one woman miscarried twice and so the couple ended up going through the insemination process three times before a pregnancy went to term.

For all of the women the insemination process raised issues that needed to be addressed. One of the first things that had to be decided was whether the recipients and donors should draw up contracts stipulating that the recipients would never pursue the donor for child support and that the donor would never assert paternity. Despite the degree of reassurance such contracts might offer to all the parties involved, many of the women were extremely uncomfortable with the notion of 'putting anything in writing.' There is no legal precedent to suggest that these contracts would stand up in a Canadian court. Further, the contract, by naming all parties involved and specifying their relationships to each other, would be an acknowledgment of an arrangement that the participants, at least initially, wished to keep private. If either the donors or the recipients decided to renege on their side of the bargain, the contract would give them proof that an arrangement existed in the first place.

Denise expressed a further reservation about contracts:

We decided that a contract did make it – You put it in writing who was involved and it might be best to let it go, because if anybody asked me, Wendy slept around. The judge is going to have to think long and hard about whether or not they're going to take DNA or whatever it is from [son] Bill's body, like actually violate Bill's body, to find out what his parentage is. So, as far as I'm concerned she slept around; we're not gay. If she has to she'll get married. I don't care what it is that we have to do ... so I think it's best left totally verbal, you know.

Thus the concern was not only that a contract would identify the donor's relationship to the recipients but also that it would identify the recipients' relationship to each other. There have been numerous court cases involving children who have been taken from lesbian mothers *because* the mothers were lesbian and thus deemed unfit.[3] Not surprisingly, then, only one of the D.I. couples used a contract, and the couple did so only at the donor's insistence.

All the women felt very strongly that the donors must never assert any paternal claim on the children. As Denise explained:

The donor will never be a parent. I mean he will never have any, um, we guaranteed him that we would never come after him for monetary or emotional support, and he can never come after us for that. Bill has two parents, and that's Wendy and myself. We're the ones who stay up at night with him. We're the ones who change his diapers. We're the ones who have devoted our paycheques to him, and we are the ones who will devote our future to him.

The idea that the child already had two parents was important to most of the women, who simply did not see a place or a necessity for the 'father' in their lives or in the life of the child.

Nonetheless, all the women felt a great deal of gratitude towards their donors. Evelyn said:

They were great. I am so impressed with these men, I can't believe it. I don't know them. We've never met ... they came through the whole time, just no question. So much compassion it was incredible.

All the anonymous donors agreed that information about themselves, including last known address and phone number, could be released to the children if they desired this information and were at least eighteen years of age. The known donors used by one couple remained friends of the family and were thus able to establish relationships with the child,

---

3 This is not to suggest that lesbian mothers are always denied custody. Jackson and Persky (1982), for example, cite three instances in Canada in which custody was awarded to homosexual parents. Unfortunately, the majority of rulings have been against homosexual parents. For further information see Gross (1986) and Arnup (1989).

but it was decided that their role would not be revealed to the child unless all four adults decided otherwise.

In considering what they would tell their children about the method they had used to become pregnant, the women decided that honesty was the best approach: they had really wanted a baby and some men had been kind enough to help them out by donating sperm. Many women felt that the probing questions of strangers ('Is his father's hair that colour?') also demanded an honest response, because they did not want to give their children the impression that there was anything wrong or embarrassing about the method of conception they had chosen.

The women expressed mixed feelings about the actual process of insemination. Several of the couples felt that it was important that both partners were involved in the insemination because it would be *their* child. Blaire, who 'inseminated Iris every time,' said it 'was important that we both be involved and that, I mean it really was making a baby together.'

The shared experience of insemination was often accompanied, in the beginning, by romantic or 'mystical' feelings. However, as time passed, these feelings tended to diminish. Iris recalled:

The first insemination – and probably the first couple – we were really romantic about it. We had herbal tea and candles and all this romantic shit, and it was really new. You know, you don't know how sperm acts. I read a lot and I knew more about sperm than I ever wanted to know, you know, sickening. If sperm was ever a category on *Jeopardy* I'd win that whole row. Yeah, so for the first few months we were really romantic and all that and then, you know, it takes a while to figure out, you know, you have to sit with your bum up in the air for a little while. And if you go to the bathroom too soon, you look down and it's all white and cloudy, and you know you've lost a good shot. So there's lots of that, there's lots of experimenting and stuff like that. We eventually became quite utilitarian about it – 'Oh, just do it, just get that stuff into me' – and started realizing that it was just going to happen whether or not we were romantic about it. We'd get really excited about how big the shot was and everything. 'Cause we'd put it into a syringe and go, 'Wow, four c.c.'s – I can't believe it.' So we managed to have quite a bit of fun about it. I'd end up, I'd plan on just lying in bed all night and Blaire would wait on me hand and foot. We'd get a movie or something and I'd watch it all night. But by the end of it, the sight of the sperm was really grossing me out. It smells like something you'd find at the bottom of a dirty garbage pail or something; it's got a really strong odour, and it reminds me of tapioca.

Evelyn related a similar experience:

Kim ended up doing it near the end just because it was becoming quite routine and I wasn't always able to be home. At first it was almost a spiritual situation. Like it was just so dramatic, being part of it and actually having it happen. It took a long time to set up the donors, maybe a year or more. So at first it was quite an emotional experience, and I had to be there and I had to do it. I was going to be a part of it. But [near the end], you know, it might happen at two in the afternoon because it was more convenient then. Or somebody might come over and visit, and I'd entertain them in the living room and Kim would be in the bedroom. You know, it's like anything. But I feel, because I was able to be supportive of the whole thing and be there, it was a good experience, a really good experience.

Iris's explanation indicates that feelings not only about the process but also about the actual sperm were often mixed. Several of the women did not like having sperm in their bodies. Many found it very strange to have sperm in their lives at all. Tina recalled:

It was very bizarre, this little vial of sperm and this syringe, and it was almost surreal, you know. And I don't know, there was something about – it was like having a third person in your bedroom, the sperm I guess, I don't know, but it was, it was pretty uncomfortable ... and I found I was quite uncomfortable about it. I was glad when it was over ... I handled it quite tactfully, but inside I wasn't all that comfortable with the process – not the process but I think just the sperm. There was something about the thought of taking someone's bodily secretions and putting it inside another person's body. I don't know, I just didn't feel comfortable about it ... I guess it was like having a stranger there because we didn't know who the sperm had come from. And it was a foreign object, you know, something that hadn't been in our house before – and there it was, in a most intimate place and situation. And yeah, I was a tad uncomfortable about it and ah, even, I mean I can talk about it and tell other women how to do it, but still there's something in the back of my mind goes 'ugh.' It's just a little 'ugh,' and a little twinge there that goes 'ugh, how strange to be handling this stuff and doing all this with this stuff, and look what you get.' I mean the results are great, but the process is a bit strange. But then, I'd never make a great nurse.

Blaire concurred:

It was kind of an unreal time in a way, looking back on it, you know, because you weren't pregnant, you know, but you had sperm around, and being lesbians you don't have sperm dropping here and there all the time. And Iris would get so sick of having sperm in her body and things like that, so there was this real sense of foreign, alien presence in a way ... Heterosexual couples would have intercourse whether they were trying to have a baby or not. For us, having sperm and inseminating Iris, we would never do that any other time than having a baby, so in a way it is kind of unreal in our whole lives as we see it. Not unreal as in 'I can't believe this is happening' but, you know, it's a moment that would never really come again, you know, for Iris, so there is that. And maybe unreal is not the best word to use, but it's [odd], very much so. Even rinsing out the syringe ... it was certainly foreign; it was certainly alien.

Many of the women experienced the insemination period as a strange limbo in which, as Blaire said, 'you're not pregnant and you're not *not* pregnant.' In this in-between time when one is neither pregnant nor not-pregnant, many women found that their lives had collapsed into a series of two-week cycles, from insemination to menstruation to ovulation and insemination again. Iris explained that

the frustrations were not so much with the method but, um, were working in two-week lots – you know, menstruation, ovulation, menstruation, ovulation. The expense of the ovulation kits, the excitement, waiting for your period to start, and being so excited and everything that, of course, your period doesn't come because you've just thrown your whole system off by thinking, 'I'm pregnant, I'm pregnant. I know I'm pregnant, I feel it. Oh, I feel morning sick, oh, I must be morning sick.' And then you go out and buy a pregnancy kit and think, 'This thing doesn't work.' Of course, you're not pregnant and your period starts the next day. That was frustrating, working in that sort of thing.

For many of the women, the two-week waiting period between insemination and menstruation was almost unbearable. Rose experienced it as 'the most strenuous time emotionally. I was not emotional through my pregnancy but that two-week period was a roller coaster.'

Several of the women said that the insemination process gave them a greater awareness of their bodies. As Rose explained, 'You're acutely aware of when your ovulation cycle is and where you are in it.' For several women this new awareness was accompanied by doubts about their physical capabilities, especially as time wore on and pregnancy was not achieved. 'It took us five months to get pregnant,' Iris recalled, and I think we really considered what if I can't pregnant, what if my body lets me down.' When I asked Iris how she would have felt if she had been unable to get pregnant, she responded:

I probably would have felt that ... I wouldn't have felt that I'm not much of a woman. I wouldn't have felt that, although I think that's what society tends to tell women who can't get pregnant, because, alas, we have a huge infertility problem. But I would have felt that my body had let me down because I wanted to be pregnant so much that I wouldn't have been able to rationalize the disappointment very well.

Some women felt a great deal of anger towards the medical industry around this time because they had been denied access to medically assisted insemination and sperm-bank sperm. But others felt that self-insemination offered advantages over medically supervised insemination. Kim said that she found self-insemination

more personal than going to the fertility clinic and getting sperm ... You know, we just did it in bed and could stay home and read a book, think of names, whatever. Very often we would just go to sleep for the night kind of thing ... It's more personal but it's also private. Not a lot of people have to know about it if you don't want.

Several of the women wanted as little interference as possible from medical practitioners, whom they frequently perceived as hostile and judgmental.

HETEROSEXUAL INTERCOURSE

Two of the women in my sample engaged in sexual intercourse for the purpose of becoming pregnant. Each decided on this course of action because she could discover no practical alternative. Each chose a man she knew and liked. Noreen told her 'donor' why she wanted to sleep with him, whereas Elly did not. And while Noreen did not tell her partner, Melanie, that she had decided to sleep with this particular man (although they had agreed that they would have children), Elly kept her partner, Nancy, informed every step of the way. Each woman was familiar enough with her cycle to be able to get pregnant after having sex only a couple of times. Noreen had two children by the same man, two and a half years apart. Elly had one child.

Although sexual intercourse was a practical solution that the couples had discussed and agreed to (at least in theory), it did present several problems for them. Since both Noreen and Elly were uncomfortable with the idea of having sex with a complete stranger, each chose a man with whom she had an emotional attachment. However, the decision to engage in an emotional and sexual relationship with a third person, even if for pragmatic reasons, threatened the lesbian relationships in the same way that having an affair might. Further, the partners felt excluded from the process of impregnation. Elly explained that Nancy was hurt not only by Elly's sexual and emotional relationship with someone else but also by her own lack of control over the process:

[I]t was *my* timetable. I met this guy, I mean we had discussed it. She was faced, in some ways she feels she was faced with an ultimatum: 'I want to get pregnant; I'm not going to do it if you don't want to.' And I was clear. I said: 'You know, I'm not going to do this without you, like we're together, this is going to be *our* whatever, but I really want to do this.' So she felt that she was blackmailed in a way. She thought maybe I'd up and leave her and go with this guy, which I was not at all going to do, and I firmly believe I would not have done it if she hadn't been with me. 'Cause there was no way I was going to be a single parent, and there was no way I was going to be, you know, get involved in a heterosexual long-term relationship with this man. So it was my agenda, and that's a problem.

Nancy related her experience of the process:

It was just something we talked about. And then I was in school and we were kind of going along, not in the greatest sort of way. And so Elly met this guy and that was sort of like 'well, Nancy, it looks like I could get pregnant,' you know, and there was a lot of pain. There was tons of pain. It was a very painful process for me. It was really painful because I had to allow Elly her feelings, you know, like she wasn't going to sleep with some guy that she didn't like, so she really truly cared for this guy on some level ... Like we hadn't been really emotionally tied. We'd been a little bit separated just because of our lives, and I had been really wrapped into my school work, like really into it, and so we'd been going along with not a lot of the really strong emotional stuff that we had been experiencing before. And for me, then I had to acknowledge that and think, 'Well, she's finding that sort of emotional need and filling it with this guy.' But we were talking through the whole process, and we knew that she could get pregnant now, and the timing was perfect. Like she's always been completely on top of when she's ovulating, and she knew she could get pregnant. She knew this was the time she was going to get pregnant if she was going to do it. I'd tell her, 'Well, do it then. Go ahead and do it. Just get pregnant if that's what you really want to do.' Because she really wanted to get pregnant. And we had talked about it, and I didn't think it was such a bad idea. Like I knew we were going to have a kid together, and so it was completely in my reality. So it's really a mix. Like I stayed home at night and I was like, I was aching. It was hard.

Elly's donor left town shortly after sleeping with her (he had only been visiting) and so never knew that Elly had become pregnant. In contrast, Noreen had to sort out some rather complex issues with her donor, an old boyfriend who had been recently divorced and left with three young children. Although he was informed of Noreen and Melanie's relationship and of Noreen's reason for sleeping with him, it became apparent to Noreen that he was hoping that once she had a child, she would leave Melanie for him. Noreen recalled the period after she had her second child by him:

He was angry then, but he'd already known, you know, the reality. And yet I was very honest with him, you know, like right from the beginning I was not leaving Melanie and I wanted a baby and he just, you know, [said] 'It's okay, it's okay.' But it was true, I mean he had three kids of his own and he wanted a mom. And it was hard 'cause I did find that I was very guilty, you know. I felt like, I think I really cared. Well, I know I cared about him, but I also I think I felt guilty about not going and being a mother to his kids. I mean he really needed somebody, but I just couldn't do it for him. So it took me a while. I probably would not have maintained – if I hadn't felt guilty I wouldn't have maintained a relationship [with him] for that long.

While Noreen knew that her donor would not claim paternity of the children (because he was already raising three children alone), Elly was, and remains, very apprehensive about her donor learning that he might have fathered a child. So concerned is she about this possibility that she has even considered moving away so that he would be unable to find her. In contrast, Noreen's donor actually had a relationship with the first child (although he saw the second child only a couple of times before he withdrew from their lives) and his parents maintained a grandparent relationship to the children until Noreen and Melanie broke their connection with them by moving to a different city.

Noreen is willing to disclose to the children the identity of their father, but neither has pursued the matter. The oldest child, a daughter who was nineteen at the time of my interview, had toyed with the idea of finding her father in her mid-teens, but never followed up on it. Noreen's explanation for this is that although the children may be curious, there is no real lack in their lives; they have always had two parents.

Choosing to get pregnant by heterosexual intercourse poses several dangers to lesbian women. The first of these is that if, like Elly, one simply seizes the opportunity when it presents itself, no kind of STD or HIV testing is possible, and no medical history can be procured. Another danger relates to the donor's intimate involvement in the insemination and with the woman. Whereas there can be a legal debate over whether a sperm donor is a 'father,' no such question pertains to a man who impregnates a woman through sexual intercourse. From a legal standpoint, this puts the women involved in a highly vulnerable position. Finally, there is the threat posed to the lesbian relationship by the involvement of one of the women with a third party. Both couples in my sample were able to resolve this conflict sufficiently to the point where they could warmly share the pregnancy, birth, and parenting.

PREGNANCY AND BIRTH

Several women experienced pregnancy or birth (or both) as an achievement. Sometimes this achievement represented a victory over a medical industry that had discouraged or been openly hostile to their pursuit of motherhood. Many women had trouble finding a doctor who would advise them during insemination and attend them through pregnancy and birth. Rose related her experiences with the physician who had been her family doctor:

I went [to see] him and said that I was in a long-term lesbian relationship – that was my first mistake – and we had decided that we wanted to have a child, and could he help me with that. He said, 'No, sorry, I can't help you with that. That's not something I believe should be done. But if that's so important, then go and stand on Third Avenue ["the stroll"] and become pregnant.' And that was his answer ... I left and I cried all the way home.

Iris explained that she and Blaire went through several doctors before finding the right one:

When we were first pregnant we had a problem because our regular doctor at the time wasn't delivering babies and she knew that we were trying to get pregnant. And when we finally went in and found out we were pregnant, she said, 'Well, you better find a doctor who'll deliver that baby.' And we had contacted a midwife who made some suggestions for a doctor who would appreciate our different outlook. And one doctor in particular told us she wouldn't deliver the baby because she didn't appreciate our lifestyle, and we were also told by a particular professional that if we wanted appropriate health care that we should lie about our situation. So we had a hard time. I mean that was really the first time ever in my life – certainly my lesbian life – that I had been so outrightly discriminated against. And it was a very vulnerable time for me, because we ended up going to a couple of different doctors. And each time, when you're at the beginning of pregnancy and you see a new doctor, you have to go for an internal exam, and I was getting really sick of opening my legs for everyone in Calgary. So it was a really frustrating time. And then finally we went to the low-risk maternity clinic at Foothills and got the treatment we deserve, and also connected with the doctor who is our family doctor now, because we liked her so much – a feminist, a good doctor.

Despite encountering some initial difficulties, each couple eventually found a doctor who accepted and encouraged them, thereby enabling them to proceed with their mission of getting pregnant and/or having a baby.

How did the women experience pregnancy, both their own and that of their partners? Some of the biological mothers were surprised to find that, having exerted enormous effort to become pregnant, they experienced guilt, confusion, or panic once they achieved their goal. This was especially so among the women who had had heterosexual intercourse for the purpose of getting pregnant. The disruption caused by their involvement with the donor had scarred the lesbian relationship and left the women trying to balance everyone's emotional needs. It was also at this point that some women started to worry about their ability to financially support a baby. Feelings ranged from mild flutters of panic to full-blown anxiety. Elly experienced the latter:

What happened after I got pregnant was I freaked out. I really, I mean I would have done anything to be pregnant, and when I was, you know, I was thrilled and then twelve hours later I freaked. I just freaked. I got terrified about money, just terrified about money. I got terrified about the fact that I felt like we weren't going to be able to do this: we were both really poor; we didn't have a house; we didn't have a car. It was like all of a sudden all my middle-class expectations of what you need to have a child, which weren't there when I was getting pregnant, suddenly they were there. Like 'Holy shit, we can't do this, we can't do this. We don't have what we need.' Money was the biggest [anxiety], security – financial security just was monumental. And if Nancy could convince me, she worked really hard at it, you know, 'Okay, Elly, we're going to have enough money.' Then I kind of went 'oh,' and *then* sort of the other stuff would come – like can I really be a parent, like am I emotionally ready to be a mother. All this stuff came up and it was really hard, very, very difficult for a couple of weeks. I was a wreck. I decided I couldn't go through with it and I made an appointment to have an abortion. I just freaked, just freaked, and as soon as I made the appointment to have an abortion then it was like 'But I want to have a baby.' I needed that choice.

Despite any initial qualms, all the women reported that pregnancy had been, overall, a positive experience for them. Several spoke of feeling very contented. A few mentioned that they had felt healthier while pregnant than at any other time. For Elly, pregnancy was a 'magical' experience:

I absolutely loved being pregnant. A magical way to be, knowing that you have another person, that you are carrying another person around, you're communicating to another person. I've never felt so wonderful, like I felt special all the time, completely special. And I *was* special, you know; it's a very special state, being pregnant. And I think there's all sorts of weird hormonal stuff that happens that makes you feel that way, extremely maternal and very careful about myself and just really wonderful, like it's just wonderful. I sometimes think of it as a gift.

One of the most enjoyable aspects of pregnancy for some women was the attention they got and the 'pampering' they received from partners, friends, and relatives. For many pregnancy was also a time of great excitement and anticipation. Iris described the effort she and her partner put into making the pregnancy a shared experience:

As I was getting bigger and bigger we shared the excitement of how big I was getting and, you know, we made maternity dresses together and all that kind of stuff, so it was just a really exciting time. She felt him kick when I was sixteen weeks pregnant and it was really exciting. It was a real time for sharing with each other, you know, because I had to explain everything explicitly so that she could understand everything, you know. It's not like I could just say to her, 'Oh, I just felt him kick,' and she would know exactly what it was, what it felt like for me. I would explain to her everything so that she could share it. She went to all my doctor's appointments with me. We were a real family that way.

Many of the biological mothers said that pregnancy gave them a new respect for their bodies or even changed their relationship to their bodies. In the words of the woman who had two miscarriages:

It's a sense of accomplishment. I did it and I'm in control and, um, I think 'cause of the miscarriages I had even more respect ... for my body and being pregnant, that I took really, really good care of myself. I ate really well and I didn't eat the junk that I wasn't supposed to. I wasn't going to take any chances on something going wrong.

Motherhood completely changed Elly's perception of her body:

I had never owned my body the way that I owned it when I was pregnant. I was never, it makes you *be* in your body. I think most of us are cut off from our bodies. We grow up to hate our bodies, especially as women, we have extremely ambivalent relationships to our bodies. And so when I was pregnant I was in my body. The centre of my universe was right here [belly] and I was in it and I was connected to it and I was a part of it, and it very much changed [my relationship to my body]. Nursing as well very much changed my relationship to my body ... Well, my breasts were no longer sex objects. They're mine, they have a purpose, they feed my baby, um, they're incredible. I mean our whole bodies are incredible. I didn't realize how incredible a uterus is, like a uterus is a muscle that pushes a big baby out a hole this big and it's your uterus that does it, one muscle in your body, it pushes a baby out a hole as big as your nose. It's phenomenal. When I was in labour I was completely at the mercy of the forces of my body. Like my body gave birth, I didn't. I was kind of watching it happen in some ways. Like some women push but I didn't, it was just my body. It was just whoosh, my body gave birth to a baby and then my body nursed it, and I mean it really changed my relationship to my body in a very positive way.

Some women described pregnancy as a time of 'coming down to earth' and preparing for the demands of motherhood that lay ahead. For Noreen, pregnancy had the somewhat sobering but ultimately positive effect of forcing her and her partner to reassess their relationship:

I think before that we just kind of expected everything to be perfect for us, you know. And then we realized that it took work, and that you had to keep trying and you had to maintain your relationship, 'cause it was important. You know, a lot of these things you just take for granted when you're young ... Especially with [the first pregnancy] we realized that there was lots that we wanted to work for and that we wanted to maintain, and we wanted to stay together. ... Like before, we just thought we'd be together forever, you know, like it wasn't even a question. But now we knew that there was some effort that had to be put into it. It just wouldn't happen like that. So that was good.

Some women spoke of a 'nesting' urge during pregnancy that motivated them to great feats of housecleaning, food preparation, and household organization in anticipation of the baby. Kim saw pregnancy as a sort of training session for motherhood:

I think the whole process is done on purpose somewhere along the line. Like whoever decided ... being pregnant and getting pregnant is related to being a mother. Like when you're pregnant you have to get up a lot in the night to go to the bathroom. I figure that prepares you for getting up in the night with a baby. You're really tired when you're pregnant, and often you're really tired when you have a baby. And, yeah, you're not so much thinking about yourself. It's just, I think, little steps toward the big end.

There is little in these accounts of pregnancy that would distinguish them from heterosexual women's experiences of pregnancy. The difference is that these pregnancies were shared with another woman, not a man. What did it feel like for a non-biological mother to go through a pregnancy that was 'hers,' but not hers in an embodied way? Nancy expressed what turned out to be a common sentiment among the non-biological mothers:

It didn't make me feel like I wanted to be the one that was pregnant. Because I *was* pregnant [too]. Elly was pregnant and so we were having a baby, and so I didn't need to be pregnant.

Although none of the non-biological mothers, in experiencing her partner's pregnancy, wanted to be the pregnant one herself, many gained a whole new respect and appreciation for women and mothers. For Nancy, pregnancy

became really an incredible thing. To watch Elly's belly grow and to feel the movement inside and to know there was a little person in there growing. Astrid

[baby] actually woke me up one night 'cause Elly and I were spooning and Astrid kicked out and I was supposed to wake up. It was time to wake up in the morning, and she woke me up – and it was pretty incredible. So that certainly was interesting ... Elly was sick a good deal of the time at the beginning – and grumpy. Like I saw pregnancy, the good and the bad. She was really into it too later on after all that [conflict] subsided, and into eating and stuff. But I never really felt like I wanted to be pregnant, even then.

Some women, intimidated by the difficulties they saw their partners go through, had mixed feelings about undergoing pregnancy later themselves if that was the agreement they and their partners had reached. By the same token, it did not seem fair to put the same partner through the ordeal a second time. Denise struggled with this quandary:

I couldn't put Wendy through the next pregnancy. I couldn't put her through that pain again ... Although the pregnancy went quite well for Wendy, I mean it's tough for a woman to go through it – the heat and the water you carry around and the weight gain, and just everything, right. And I think that it's only fair that I be the one to try for the second one. You know, I don't think it would be fair of me just to blanket, flat out say no, you know. And so I'm going to go for it and have the second one, and then Wendy can have the third.

Although it was an eye-opening experience, each of the non-biological mothers reported that she enjoyed the pregnancy and was able to share in the excitement of it. One woman, who had given birth during a previous heterosexual relationship, went so far as to say, 'This is the best way to have a baby [let your partner have it]. I'm not kidding.'

Each couple said that pregnancy had an effect on their relationship.[4] Many were drawn closer together as they began their transition into a family. For many couples, the fact that the non-biological mother had to become more attentive to the biological mother's needs during pregnancy represented a shift from their prior equality with respect to roles. Blaire and her partner experienced this shift as a challenge:

I mean I certainly felt challenged that I had to do more taking care of and not

---

4 One aspect of the relationships that I did not pursue was the sexual realm. In retrospect, I think it would have been worth exploring how sexual relations were negotiated around pregnancy and mothering, and how mothers dealt with issues of intimacy in light of all the new demands on their time and energy. This would be an interesting question for future research.

expect to be taken care of the same back, um, do more physical things around the house. Which of course made me feel good, made me feel, 'Oh yeah, I can clip the whole bloody hedge' ... She had to really adjust to not being able to do the things that she would normally do. And she really likes physical work, and she would do gardening things at eight-months' pregnant, and I'd have a hard time accepting that. So I think that was the main change, was just that caring for change. And then, you know, moments of not being aware of what she needed, you know, tripping me up kind of thing, but nothing really traumatic, nothing big-time.

Tina related a similar experience:

I tended to be more domestic for Rose, you know, and assumed a lot of the roles, the chores that she did. But because her pregnancy was quite easy, she carried on pretty well the way she had normally done. The only difference was I had to tie up her shoes for her. I think it really brought us closer together. We became quite a unit, you know, and I didn't feel excluded from the pregnancy at all.

Many of the couples reported that pregnancy changed how they were perceived by other people. Most of the women found that pregnancy or the presence of a child leads strangers to assume that they are, or have been, in a heterosexual relationship. In this respect, pregnancy can make the lesbian relationship even more invisible than it had previously been.

Many of the women were struck by the lesbian community's response to the pregnancy. A few said that pregnancy seemed to symbolize for the community an affirmation of the couple's commitment to each other. 'I think it made it quite clear that this is a permanent relationship,' Kim said. 'Like it was a visual commitment, and people could see ... like there was no doubt.' The language denoting heterosexual relationships – 'going out,' 'going steady,' 'becoming engaged,' 'shacking up,' 'getting married,' and so forth – cannot generally be used to describe lesbian relationships. Lesbian women have neither the language nor, for the most part, the practices that mark the various stages and types of relationships they may be having. Thus we can see why a couple's pursuit of pregnancy could be so meaningful to the lesbian community. The lack of institutional support, as expressed in the dearth of special terms and practices, lends a certain fluidity and fragility to lesbian relationships; in such a context, pregnancy becomes a concrete statement.

Several women felt that some members of the lesbian community also saw them as 'pioneers' who were proving that it is possible for lesbians to have babies. Blaire commented:

Our friends in the lesbian community saw it as a strength of our relationship. Maybe in a little way in awe about us doing it, as if, 'Gee, you just went ahead and did it. I mean, lesbians want to do this – I'd like to have kids. But geez, you're doing it.' So there was this, it was this wonderful embracement and support and, you know, 'anything we can do' and 'tell me about it' kind of thing.

Related to the perception that the couple were now truly committed to each other was the perception that the couple and the child were a 'family' in a way the couple had not been before the child came along. Some women felt that the opposite was true – that there was no place in the conventional conception of family for *two* mothers, and so the non-biological mother became conceptually displaced. Tina explained:

There's a tendency to think of [the lesbian family] as the mother-and-child and her partner. So there is a separation there. And that goes on in the lesbian community too. They tend to think of mother-child as one unit, you know. But I think that's changing because we're seeing more and more lesbian families, so it's just a matter of the education process.

Another issue that tended to emerge during pregnancy was the role of the extended family. The pregnancy forced many women's parents and siblings to be more forthright in acknowledging and dealing with the lesbian relationship than they had been in the past. This was sometimes quite problematic. 'As soon as a person comes out of the closet,' Evelyn observed, 'everybody around them goes into one.' Some couples withdrew from their families during pregnancy to avoid hostility and conflict.

Other families, especially those of the biological mothers, became very involved in the pregnancy, and occasionally very possessive of their daughter and grandchild. Their concerns about lesbian mothering were sometimes manifested in the form of an overprotectiveness that became intrusive or threatening to the lesbian couple. Wendy's mother made it clear that if anything should happen to Wendy, Wendy's parents would try to take the baby away from Denise (because biologically it was *theirs*). This threat upset the couple tremendously, Wendy recalled:

The whole time I was pregnant we were more concerned about what would happen if I was dead than concentrating on the fact that there was something fabulous happening here, you know. And I don't know, I sort of lived through the pregnancy with this morbid fear.

It took a great deal of time and effort to persuade Wendy's parents to acknowledge Denise as Bill's other parent, with equal parental rights.

Many of the women received more support from friends than family during their pregnancy. This was the experience of the couple who had two miscarriages. As the non-biological mother recounted:

Friends were really supportive, and well not necessarily our gay friends, our straight friends too ... They were there and you could tell that they felt the pain too and knew what we were going through. But no family, they weren't there. My mom wasn't negative. She was hoping that we wouldn't be interested in doing it again. But she'd come up with stuff like 'Well, maybe it's for the best.' But again, she's 82; it comes from her upbringing. I mean those were things that were said to every woman who had a miscarriage. So I think they [family] were really quite relieved after that; they didn't really have to tell anyone.

Blaire and her partner had a similar experience. 'Our parents and all our siblings were important, but really it was us, you know. And lots of support from friends. Overwhelming support from friends.'

Evelyn had an interesting explanation for why families and acquaintances, apart from their discomfort with lesbianism, might treat pregnant and mothering lesbian couples with less respect than they would treat heterosexual couples:

My perception of it is that we learn etiquette and people just don't know etiquette with us. We've got to tell them what etiquette is. And when they know how to be polite with us, they will be polite. But nobody has ever told anyone how to be polite around a lesbian.

Whether it is a matter of etiquette or fundamental ideological differences, families were often simply not available to their pregnant lesbian daughters as they were or would be to their heterosexual daughters. Thus, for all couples, friends were of the utmost importance. For Nancy and her partner, they constituted a new extended family:

Our close friends really drew in and they became aunties. It's like it created an extended sort of family with a lot of our friends. Astrid has many aunties.

Conflicts with the mothers' relatives often subsided somewhat after the birth, when family members either accepted the baby or refused to acknowledge that the baby had anything to do with them or their daughter.

Another issue that emerged during pregnancy concerned the selection of the baby's last name. Two of the couples decided that the baby would have the surnames (hyphenated) of both mothers. To accomplish this, the biological mother had to change her name to the hyphenated form, because a baby must have the same surname as its mother if it does not have a father. Other couples chose to wait until future children were born and then change the parents' and children's names *en masse*.

Pregnancy was also a time that required on the part of the mothers a great deal of contact – and frequently intimate contact – with medical personnel. As discussed earlier, several women had difficulty finding physicians who could comfortably attend them during pregnancy and birth. Once suitable doctors were found, however, further difficulties of this sort were minimal.

The women who attended pre-natal classes were met with enthusiasm and friendliness from the instructors and often from the other participants. It was sometimes awkward, however, when the participants were asked to split into two groups – mothers and fathers – and the non-biological mothers had to go with the fathers. Wendy said that even though she shared some common concerns with prospective fathers, and thus found it interesting to speak with them, she was *not* a father, was not seen as a father, and yet was not acknowledged as a mother. Once again, we see that in the conventional mother-child and mother-father-child patterns, the non-biological mother is left invisible, struggling to secure and define her role.

Nancy faced a similar problem at the birth – a home birth – itself:

At one point the midwife told me I needed to shift positions and come away from Elly and be there in a different way for Elly. Like I had been there with her breathing and so *there* with her that the midwife kind of called me back and said, you know, like saying, 'You're not giving birth so you have to be there supporting her through birth.' Which was kind of shocking in a way.

But maybe Nancy *was* giving birth. She had stated earlier that if Elly was pregnant then *she* was pregnant, so perhaps if Elly was giving birth, Nancy was giving birth too. By 'calling back' Nancy, it is possible that the midwife was responding to this couple in the same way she responded to heterosexual couples, without considering that perhaps two women can give birth differently than a man and woman generally do.

Apart from Noreen and Melanie, who had their children twenty years ago when family members generally were not allowed in the delivery room, all the couples went through labour and birth together. All found the hospital staff extremely encouraging. Each non-biological mother was acknowledged as the partner and co-parent and was given a pass-card (which was normally given to fathers) to enter the nursery.

The women spoke of birth as an intense and exhilarating shared experience. The moving account given to me by Blaire and Iris was typical. Blaire was with Iris (the biological mother) through the labour and was holding her as birthing began. When Blaire felt the pain Iris was in, she began to cry. When Iris looked up at Blaire and felt Blaire's distress, she worried about Blaire and wondered how she could endure seeing Blaire go through this ordeal at the next birth. On an emotional level, they inhabited each other's bodies as this birth also became future births and somewhere in the middle of it all the *two of them* gave birth to their son.

The births were greeted with feelings of exhilaration and triumph. Wendy recalled:

I had never felt so special, and so – what's the word for it – like I had accomplished, like I could be proud of myself for accomplishing something that I did the first week after he was born. And everybody makes you feel special too.

Of course, birth is just the beginning of motherhood, as Wendy acknowledged:

Basically, motherhood starts the day the child is born. This business of being pregnant and giving birth is not motherhood, it's something entirely different. I don't know what it is.

Becoming a mother is one thing; *being* a mother is quite another.

4

Achieving Motherhood:
Blended Families

Some women in my sample followed the traditional route to mother-hood; they were married or involved in relationships with men, and either way eventually became pregnant. Most of these women had shared parenting with their male partners for some part of their children's lives. Of the fifteen women in my Group B sample, ten had become mothers in this manner. Becoming a mother, however, is not the same as becoming a *lesbian* mother. The latter role was frequently shared with other mothers or with one of the five other members of Group B who had not previously had children.

Group B women thus comprised a number of different family configurations. Of the six couples, four consisted of one biological mother and one woman who had not previously mothered. In the other two couples, both women were biological mothers when they entered the relationship. Of the three single women, two were single mothers. The third woman had previously been in two separate relationships in which she had played a step-parenting role. In one of these relationships the child had been conceived during a prior heterosexual relationship, while in the other the child had been conceived during a prior lesbian relationship.

My focus here is on the process of becoming a lesbian mother. For many of the women in Group B, that process occurred simultaneously with becoming involved in a lesbian relationship. Frequently, the biological mothers were discovering the *lesbian* aspect of lesbian mother-hood, whereas the previously childless women were discovering the *motherhood* aspect of it. Although single mothering is not my focus, the two single mothers were included in the sample because they came to identify themselves as lesbian external to an involvement in a lesbian relationship. Their accounts of this process thus supplement the information I received from the other women.

Since the children were already present, the process of becoming a lesbian mother was fundamentally different from that experienced by the Group A women. The focus of this chapter, then, is the process by which blended lesbian families were formed and by which each woman, whether previously a mother or not, became a lesbian mother. Creating these families was no easy task, though all the women believed that they would have faced at least some of the same challenges had they been trying to form a heterosexual blended family. At the same time, they also felt there were obstacles that only lesbian women would face in the blended-family context.

One of the biggest problems facing these families is the absence of an accepted set of labels for key activities and roles. This is also a problem for external observers who wish to discuss them. That the biological mothers are mothers is fairly straightforward. But what do we call the second woman, who is also playing a parental role? In our society the sort of parenting women do is *mothering* whereas the sort of parenting men do is *fathering*, and we assume that the two of them operate together. A woman who gets involved with a man and his children has a ready-made role and label. But 'stepmother' does not accurately describe lesbian women in this position, and 'stepfamily' does not accurately describe their families. Nonetheless, I will refer to the second woman as the stepmother because, even though it is not completely accurate, it is the best term we have at this time. I also use this term because it is often necessary to distinguish these women from the biological mothers. As we shall see, this is a problem with which the women themselves struggle.

DECIDING TO BLEND

The first step, after the couples had met and knew they wanted to be together, was to decide if they could (or even wanted to) integrate their previously separate lives into a new and functioning family unit. For women who were not mothers, often the first question was whether or not they wanted to be involved with children, regardless of what their role with the children might become. Each acknowledged that her partner and her partner's children were 'a package deal.' In deciding whether or not to pursue involvement, these women had to scrutinize their complex feelings about children, relationships, and motherhood. Daphne recalled:

I've always been in a relationship with one other person – not that you can always be considered adult and mature, but a little more mature than kids – and I don't know really what I thought. I mean Sharon and I had known each other all these years, and we had a friendship – and I thought about it, you know. I mean I spent enough time over at the house, and I'd seen the kids. And they're nice kids, but I thought, 'God, could I live with kids?' I had an abortion when I was younger and I always kind of wished that I'd had children. I had this feeling that I hadn't kind of fulfilled my life dreams without a child. And when I had my abortion I got an infection so I couldn't physically have children. And I feel part of my longing was, you know, when you can't have something, you want it. And I suspect that even if I'd had the choice I probably would have chosen not to.

Some women were wary of getting involved with another woman's children to whom they would have no legal claim. They were very aware of the danger of allowing themselves to become emotionally involved with children with whom they might lose all contact if the relationship between the two women ended. For this reason, many needed to be confident of the longevity of the relationship before they made a commitment to it.

This same caution was exercised by the biological mothers, who were often unwilling to ask a woman to play a major role in their children's lives if they believed there was a chance that the relationship would dissolve after the children had formed attachments to the newcomer. Some biological mothers also said they were more careful about choosing partners than they had been when they had no children:

I found getting involved with Carol I was much more careful about who I was getting involved with and to what extent ... because of the kids. And I really was thinking, 'You know, you're not going to involve somebody here who could hurt the kids in any way' ... and guilt and stuff too ... And then one day it dawned on me – why had I not been that careful for myself?

Most of the biological mothers had been single mothers for some time before becoming involved in a new relationship. Only one had previously been involved in a lesbian blended family. Some women were concerned about the tremendous change that the new arrangement would bring to their children's lives. 'I knew it was going to be weird because we had never lived with anyone before,' Tracy said. 'So it was going to be a big adjustment in our lives, for all of us.' Other women were concerned about how their children would deal with a new set of siblings, and how they would resolve issues of territoriality. Janine's biggest concern was

blending the family ... introducing. Having a twelve and almost fifteen-year-old and then introducing a three-year-old. And boundary issues all involved with that – you know, who's going to sleep where, what would be Nicki's room. And that sort of spilled over into sharing things.

Such concerns are not unusual for a woman contemplating having a relationship with a person (male or female) who has children, or for a mother considering involvement with another person or parent. There were some concerns, however, that were specifically linked to the lesbian relationship that was being entered. For most of the biological mothers, this was either their first lesbian relationship or the first time they had brought a lesbian relationship into their homes. It was thus at this time that some of the women came out to their children. Although reactions varied, many of the children were upset at first. Janine described what happened when she came out to her teenaged daughter and son.

Initially, Jancy didn't seem bothered by it, but I think it was more that she was in stunned silence. Scott was very upset ... You know, all the concerns went through their minds ... Does that mean I will be too? What will my friends think? How do I tell people? *Do* I tell people? Why are you doing this to me? Why can't you just be like other moms?

Michelle's two teenaged daughters had similar sorts of questions.

Are you going to tell anybody? Are you going to have somebody living here? Are you sure that you are [lesbian]? Are my friends going to know? It is just really gross. Are you going to be kissing in front of us? Are you going to be sleeping with somebody?

Michelle summed up her children's response:

They were angry, really, really, upset ... They were angry that I was different than all their friends' parents I think is the bottom line ... They weren't overly concerned that there wasn't going to be a man in the house. There hasn't been one there for years.

Only five of the sixteen children involved were twelve years of age or younger when the transition to blended family occurred. The rest were teenagers who had developed some firm ideas and feelings about lesbianism and its social acceptability. Although the children were able to come to terms with the *idea* of lesbianism rather quickly, the *fact* of lesbianism in their homes was quite another matter, as we shall see later in the chapter. The concerns about 'difference' – both their mothers' and their own (because of their mothers) – were not easily resolved. Many of the mothers (both biological and stepmothers) shared their children's concerns that they would be ridiculed or ostracized for having lesbian mothers. This was an issue that could not be neatly resolved at this time; in fact, it remained a concern after the families formed.

For some biological mothers, the fact that it was a lesbian relationship they were bringing into the home was distinctly positive. Trish felt that her children could only benefit from her relationship with Andrea:

It was a loving, non-abusive, supportive relationship, the total opposite of what I had with my kids' dad. So I felt it could do them nothing but good. To see two people that really loved each other and cared about each other and really respected each other, and, you know, the other person could actually *do* what they wanted to. That sort of thing.

Trish believed that she would be able to have this sort of healthy relationship only with another woman.

Clearly, deciding whether to attempt to create a new family was no light undertaking. Careful consideration had to be given not only to the relationship between the women but also to the relationships with and between children. For those women who had never been involved with children before, the prospect was sometimes daunting. Equally daunting was the fact that many of the women, biological mothers or not, simply could not fully anticipate what they were getting into. Carol said that the concerns she had when she was deciding whether to move in with Laura and Laura's children

[were] much less than the reality proved, actually. If I had known all that I was getting into I don't know if I would have done it. And that would have been a shame I think. Um, I don't think I had a clue, looking back. I thought I did, um, at the time. I know I sat down with myself and had a little [think] ... One of the things I considered is, you don't get in and out as easily or as quickly when there's kids involved. I needed to really think about this ... But yeah, in hind-

sight I didn't know what to think about while I was thinking of it, you know. It's about a million times harder than I thought it would be. At least a million times harder.

It is impossible to know how many lesbian women grapple with their concerns and decide against step-parenting or blending their families. For the women in my sample who decided they would do it, the decision was but the beginning of what would prove to be one of the greatest challenges of their lives.

STEP-PARENTING ISSUES

Attempting to blend two separate families, or a family and an individual, presented a great many challenges to the women I interviewed. All the women stated that at least some of the issues they had to deal with would have been the same had they been in a heterosexual relationship.

One area that generated an often unexpected amount of disagreement between the two women was that of parenting styles and priorities. Many of the couples found it difficult to reconcile two different parenting approaches. This was true whether biological mothers were involved with other biological mothers or with women who had never mothered before. Women who were already mothers had an established style of mothering that, of course, no other woman could match exactly. Those who were new to mothering were sometimes surprised to find that they also had strong ideas about mothering and did not always agree with how their new partners did it. Women who had not previously been involved with children were frequently surprised, even distraught, at the central role the children played in their mothers' lives. Tracy, a biological mother, described the situation with Barbara, who had previously been child-free:

There's things about my parenting style that Barbara doesn't agree with. Um, she thinks I lend Lorna too many of my things. And things that Barbara buys me I sometimes lend my daughter and they sometimes get lost, which really, really irritates Barbara ... She thinks I'm too lenient sometimes. [Or] not lenient – because I'm really not lenient – but, um, I think she thinks that I do too much for Lorna. I drive her too many places. I bake things for the school. I do all these things, and she says Lorna should be more accommodating to us and our schedules, and we should only drive her if it's convenient to us. And I sort of have the attitude 'Well, she's a kid, I'm the parent, and I'll do whatever I can.' So I'm more willing to bend over backwards than Barbara is. She thinks Lorna takes advantage of me ... I think Barbara feels that I've been a parent so long and at too young of an age, and it probably makes her sad that I didn't have time to discover myself more and not have so much responsibility all the time.

Like Barbara, many of the previously childless women had accepted the *idea* of parenthood, but were shocked when faced with the multitude of tasks that parenting involves.

Some of the previously childless women found the parenting styles of their partners incomprehensible and almost impossible to tolerate. Daphne felt that Sharon's daughter, Kandy, had been raised far too leniently:

Kandy got what Kandy wanted and so a monster had been created by the age of twenty, because this kid had gotten what she wanted all the time. And Sharon felt guilty that she had divorced and guilty because she had gone out to work and hadn't been there for the kids. And so with all this guilt, you know, Kandy was just ruling the roost. And then I came in. And I came from a background where – and I'm not saying it was right, I know it wasn't right – but my grandmother brought me up and she was a disciplinarian, and so it was almost intolerable for me to have this kid running the household.

Often the newcomer was reluctant to 'rock the boat' by criticizing her partner's parenting skills. As Daphne went on to explain:

I found I was quite compromising and stuff at the beginning because I didn't want to make any waves, and so I ended up in therapy. And I spent a lot of time in therapy talking about Kandy.

Another woman said:

You don't want to talk to mothers about their children. No matter how good the relationship, you don't talk to them about their children. I learned that the hard way.

As difficult as it was for the newcomers to comment on what they felt was problematic parenting, it was also difficult for the biological mothers to know that someone was watching them parent – and with a critical eye. Sharon said:

There's been lots of difficulties with me bringing in another adult, but not necessarily related to her being a woman ... I really struggled a lot with 'Here's somebody. Am I doing it right?' There's somebody there all of a sudden watching
you be a parent. And there's, plus, I mean we did disagree on a lot of things.
And Daphne didn't have any experience in the fact that things pass. It all looked
pretty crisis-looking to her. And I would not act on a lot of stuff that she would
be just going through hell over, because I'm not a very, I'm a fairly laid-back
kind of person.

Sharon was not the only woman who was frustrated by her partner's
inexperience with parenting. Several of the new stepmothers were
equally frustrated with their own lack of knowledge about children and
had to struggle to establish their own niche of authority within the house.
This sometimes proved to be extremely contentious, however, when biological mothers found themselves reluctant to share authority that had
once been solely theirs. Many of these mothers noted that their children
were also unwilling to accept another authority figure in their lives.
When Christine and Janine moved in together, Christine had a three-
year-old son, Nicki, and Janine had two teenagers. Christine explained
that she did not share the parenting of Nicki with Janine because

Nicki just wouldn't allow it. And in some ways I wouldn't allow it either. He
was mine and I wasn't prepared to share him with anybody. I had a complete
set of ideas on how I wanted him raised, how he was going to be handled. And
it really contradicted [Janine's view of] how children should be raised. And I
think if we were to go back now I wouldn't change a whole lot of what I did. I'd
probably be a little more consistent like she was – 'cause I'm paying the price
now – but I don't think I would have given her much more latitude at the time.
Now, because Nicki's bigger [age ten] and our lives are different, he has to
accept parenting out of her, because she's not going away. And I've got to the
point where I don't want to do it all any more. It's too tiring.

Janine added that, since they were both mothers, they were

two authorities butting heads ... You know, I know best for my kids, you know best
for your kids. Or [just] I know best. It's hard perhaps being in a relationship where
both people think they know best. And certainly that's been an ongoing issue.

In most of the families, the biological mother retained primary
authority over her children and had the final decision-making power. It

was thus necessary for the second adult to figure out where and how she could fit into the family. Several women found it quite difficult to determine who the second adult could be, if not a parent. 'It's really hard being in a relationship where you're the other adult but you're not the parent,' Ellis said. 'It's a real tough tough role to play. It's hard for both of us to play that role.'

Because many of the children were teenagers, several women said that a parenting role would not have been appropriate for them anyway. What they hoped for, and what they strove to establish, was a relationship wherein they were considered an 'older friend.' Some of the couples found, however, that it was still necessary for them to overcome their own and their children's reluctance to accept another authority figure and to find some way to 'co-parent.' Christine explained that she and Janine needed outside help to make this transition:

We're co-parenting now. And I think that's the lesson we learned. [The therapist] made us look at [the question] 'Are you co-parenting or are you single-parenting? Decide what it's going to be because as long as the kids get a double message, they've got you.' And we needed to survive these kids, so it became very much 'Okay, we have to cooperate.' And I may not like how Janine handles him sometimes, but I keep my nose out of it. 'Cause if Nicki knows I'm going to jump in and defend him, or say 'that's wrong,' or belittle her in front of him, he's got it made. And I refuse to. There are times I have to sit on my hands or leave the room 'cause I don't agree with what's going on but if she's handling it, [I let her] just do it.

There was no abuse 'going on' here, but Christine and Janine, like several of the other women, found it very difficult to relinquish authority over their own children to another person who would handle critical situations differently than they would themselves.

As mentioned earlier, the biological mothers were not the only ones who had difficulty dealing with a new parental figure in the house. The children themselves often firmly resisted the authority of the newcomer, and although their resistance generally abated over time, sometimes it did not. Nor was accepting the authority of a new 'parent' the only aspect of the blended family that many children found problematic. Several of the biological mothers explained that their children, accustomed to living in a single-parent household, were unwilling the share their mothers with other people. Tracy described her daughter's response when Barbara moved in with them:

There was the usual jealousy [about] someone else in my life, 'cause there hadn't been someone in my life for a really long time. But I don't think it was any worse than with boyfriends. I actually think it was better because I was happy and she could tell that.

Some women believed that part of their children's resistance to a new parental figure had to do with their unwillingness to accept their mother as a sexual being. Sharon commented:

That was another issue that we [she and her twenty-year-old daughter, Kandy] never talked about. To deal with the fact that your mother is a sexual being, especially when I hadn't really been with anybody for as long as she could remember. Besides, your mother doesn't do any of that kind of stuff. So that was tough and we really kind of pushed it, trying to push it at the right speed that she could accept it and understand. And I think Daphne was pretty good about that, eh. She was pretty direct and said, 'You know, your mom is a sexual being and you're going to have to deal with that.' So that makes a relationship hard.

Children of 'unbroken' marriages might never have to acknowledge a parent's sexuality so directly.

Between trying to establish and maintain her relationship with her new partner and maintain a reasonably peaceful relationship with her children, a biological mother could easily feel caught in the middle as she tried to juggle everyone's emotional needs. Sharon said:

Kandy's a very strong individual, and I think Daphne and Kandy had all sorts of dynamics going on and were triggering each other, and there was this stuff [conflict] going on. And I ended up in the middle of all that.

Trish found herself in a similar situation:

I always feel like I'm in the middle. If it wasn't for me – well, it's logical, nobody would be in this situation together. I mean I've got my kids and there's Andrea [partner], and I really feel like I'm the anchor. And I'm getting sick of that role. You know, I don't want to be the anchor.

Biological mothers, especially those in relationships with childless women, often felt overwhelmed by everyone's demands on their time and energy. Andrea commented:

That's an issue that we haven't really resolved yet. Because I want her [Trish's] attention, but she feels needed [in] all these areas. She doesn't want anybody's attention. She just wants to be left alone. You know, like she wants some space.

The problem is that the new adult, if childless, is involved in a primary relationship with her partner only (at least at first) while the partner is involved in primary relationships with everyone – children and lover. Ellis explained:

I think part of the tension for me is I wanted the relationship, I didn't want the kids. But it's a package deal ... and there's a whole pile of ramifications to that ... Likely the vast majority of the conflict that we've had in our relationship revolves around the kids.

The imbalance of emotional involvements that exists between the biological mother and her childless partner can make the mother the most popular individual in the house while marginalizing the new partner.

Emotional imbalance is not the only aspect of the blended family that the stepmothers found troublesome. 'Getting together' often meant moving into the home of the biological mother and her children because usually the single woman did not live in a place large enough to accommodate them all. Thus the new partner was not only moving into the family's emotional network, she was also moving into their physical space, their structure and routines, and their traditions.

Not surprisingly, many women felt excluded from their new families. After moving into Sharon's house, Daphne said,

it took me a long time before I was comfortable. I never felt at home. And especially with Kandy making sure that I didn't feel at home, it was a long time before I ... I think it was six months before I actually felt that ... And I don't really think that Kandy intentionally wanted me to feel that way. I think she felt pretty badly when I finally talked to her about that ... But it *was* their home and they have certain ways of doing things and places they put things. It's bad enough when you're with one person and they have a place they put a knife. I know that I have my own little quirks that I've had to just throw to the wind, because I can't just walk into someone else's house and start establishing my own quirks. But one day I unloaded the dishwasher and I put the tall glasses on the left and the little glasses on the right and, you know, it was like Kandy opened the cupboard and it was just like 'What the hell is going on here?' And it was like this criminal offence had taken place, and that hurt me because it was like, you know, I don't have a place.

The biological mothers were usually aware of their partners' feelings of exclusion, but often felt there was only so much they could do to mitigate those feelings. Tracy had this to say about Barbara and the relationship that Tracy had with her daughter, Lorna:

I think at first she did [feel left out] when she realized how close Lorna and I were. There's things that her [Lorna] and I share that no one could ever ever be included in, just because we've lived our lives together, for twelve years. Yeah, I think she [Barbara] has accepted that Lorna and I have a bond and it's something special that she'll never be a part of, you know. I accept that too. I don't include Barbara in everything. I do things with Lorna that don't include Barbara. And we need that. We need a minimum amount of time together, just my daughter and I, for everything to run smoothly.

There were other aspects of family life that the new mothers had not anticipated. Many were surprised by the lack of privacy there is in a household populated by children, especially children who are used to having an intimate relationship with their mother. Because many of the biological mothers had been single for quite some time, there had been no need for any kind of 'closed-door policy' in their homes. Many of the incoming partners found it extremely bothersome that children felt free to walk unannounced into bedrooms and bathrooms. Not only space but also belongings, were shared. It was often difficult for the newcomers to adjust to all the sharing, especially if they had been living alone. Sharon commented:

I guess that one of the biggest things [about] moving in there was, um, everything's always been mine, my house, my car. Even when you're living with another adult. But God, when you move in with kids, *nothing* is your own. Everything is community property.

Some women were surprised at the amount of money it takes to maintain a family, especially one with teenagers. And some discovered, unfortunately, that they simply did not like their partners' children.

Although no family faced all these problems, none made the transition to blended family without facing at least a few of them. I asked the women if they thought the situation would have been different if they had moved in with a male partner. Janine's response was typical:

Well, somewhat I think in that they had to deal with the lesbian issue. They were thrust into having to deal with something that they would never have had to. Most of it, no. I still believe that most of it we would have gone through anyway. You know, if it had been a man moving in with his three-year-old son, the issues would still have been there. You know, parenting and who takes care [of whom] and 'they don't have any authority over me' kind of issues, and 'who's this little twerp of a three-year-old getting into my toys?' Absolutely, I think those issues would have been there regardless.

Many of these are standard step-parenting problems; from 'the lesbian issue' stemmed another set of problems.

LESBIAN STEPFAMILIES

That it was lesbian relationships in which their mothers were engaging raised a variety of issues for the children in the families. As discussed earlier, many of the children were initially shocked to learn of their mothers' lesbianism. Some children found the idea of lesbianism unpalatable, while others had difficulty reconciling it with the religion in which they had been raised. Ultimately, however, it was not the idea of lesbianism that was so problematic for these children – it was its presence in their homes. Michelle revealed that her daughters had become reconciled to the fact of her lesbianism but were not necessarily ready to be told that their mother was involved in an actual lesbian relationship. Michelle said:

I don't think they would have liked any woman I went out with, though ... because then they're going to have to admit that mom *is* a lesbian. I mean she's [only] hanging around with them right now, but she hasn't got a girlfriend. But if she came home with a girlfriend it could get tense. Rachel told Riley the other day that if mom ever did get a girlfriend [Rachel would] move out. And I have a hard time with that.

More than one mother was told by her child, 'I don't want any funny stuff happening in the house.' Whether the children were objecting to lesbian sexuality or to the idea of their mothers as sexual beings is unclear. At least two of the biological mothers suggested, after their lovers moved in with them, that perhaps they should abstain from sexual relations until the children left home (some years in the future). This suggestion was never well received, and the mothers were forced to reconsider.

Part of the discomfort many children felt with respect to their mothers living openly as lesbians stemmed from their own fear of ostracism. Most of the couples empathized with their children's concerns, and often felt guilty for 'burdening' them. Like many couples, Nanette and Ellis tried to 'keep a low profile' so their children could lead 'normal' lives. Nanette explained:

One of [daughter] Nina's friends knows that I'm a lesbian. She is open with her, but that girl doesn't come to our house. They don't bring their friends home. They don't want people to know that we're gay. They don't want to be teased ... So they're not open. I mean who would blame them, for heaven's sake, when 'normal' is pushed down our throats every day, with television and school. And the teachers are just as much to blame with what is normal and what is not ... But I know it's not easy having lesbian parents. They don't want their friends to know, because they don't want to suffer. And who can blame them? I mean if we'd just *come out* and get it over with, I guess their true friends would rise to the top.

Several women felt guilty that their lesbianism 'closeted' their children by requiring them to exercise great caution when revealing to outsiders the circumstances of their home lives. Some were willing to take whatever steps were necessary to protect their children from the negative attitudes about lesbianism that prevail in Canadian society. Nanette said:

I don't really have to live in the closet. I could come out if I wish to come out. But the children do not have the defences yet, are not strong enough emotionally to face the fear of being out, and what that fear means to them. Even if it's just a deep breath and everything goes on as usual. Nobody's ready to face that yet. By the time they're twenty-one or so, twenty-two, have their separate identities, can really securely see themselves as separate identities, I think then ... We will do whatever needs to be done for the kids to be comfortable ... They're afraid of the unknown. And I don't want them to be ostracized, and I don't want to be ostracized by blatant openness that isn't really necessary. I don't want to be known by my sexuality. I want to be known by who I am as a person and the quality of the person I am. I don't think it's necessary to be that 'out.'

Lesbianism was not always such an overt cause of problems. For example, lesbian relationships tend to be emotionally intense, carrying the potential of an emotional 'fusion' or 'mergence' of the two partners (Nichols 1987: 107). This is especially true in one's first lesbian relationship, which is what many of these women were encountering. They reported an emotional intensity quite unlike any they might have experienced in their relationships with men. Such intensity was sometimes threatening to the children. Daphne stated that her children seemed more upset by the deep friendship she had with Sharon than by the fact that they were lovers. It seemed to some couples that the emotional intimacy between the women left the children feeling that they had to compete with their stepmothers for the emotional attentions of their biological mothers.

Some women also sensed that their daughters were more threatened by a strong lesbian relationship than they would be by a similar heterosexual one. Laura, among others, speculated that this might be because girls believe they can be more easily displaced by another female than by a male:

Maybe for my daughter there was more of a threat because it's another woman, whereas she's my only daughter, right, so this is kind of a special relationship. Maybe that's why Dan [son] was less problem. He *is* the only man in my life ... He likes that role ... For a short time I did live with a man before I came out and Dan was very jealous.

Another intimacy issue was experienced by the incoming partners. As mentioned earlier, many felt uncomfortable with the lack of privacy in the household. It is possible that the children, most of whom were female, were more likely to take certain liberties with a stepmother than with a stepfather. Accustomed to largely (if not exclusively) female company, it is possible that they did not give much thought to, for example, walking into the bathroom when the stepmother was there, whereas they might not have done so as readily were a stepfather involved.

One of the biggest problems facing lesbian stepfamilies has to do with terminology. There is no name for the second adult. She is not a 'stepmother' as we tend to use that term; nor is she, strictly speaking, a 'mother,' since the children already have one. Having no name can mean having no identity. 'I feel I have become kind of an unidentified entity,' Barbara said. She elaborated:

I call it no-name-brand parenting. You have, um, you have neither the role nor the definition nor the relationship, and I think what the result of that was is it made me realize that if there was to be a relationship there that *I* would have to determine what that was.

Janine said that she was not a 'step-parent' to Christine's son, Nicki; rather, she was a 'parental figure.' I asked her to describe the difference between the two:

Societal recognition. It's one thing for a second marriage to happen and an opposite-sex pair to walk into the family. Because there are groups connected with that. There are support systems, there is literature written about it – although there is *some* about lesbian relationships but not nearly enough – and there's societal recognition. If Christine had been a man that had moved into my home and had lived here for seven years, the assumption, whether we were married or not legally, would be that we were partners. We would be treated as such. And the expectation is if, um, if someone called with something with regards to Nicki's education or whatever, inviting him to a birthday party, then that parent would assume that I was a co-parent and would give me equal information and ask me equal questions, respect my opinion equally. They don't. 'Cause they don't see me as an equal parent. So it's really hard to reconcile it for yourself when, in fact, society doesn't even recognize it.

In those rare cases in which the child had a father with whom he or she had a relationship, the role of the second woman became even more problematic, especially given that she was attached to the mother instead of the father. In a sense, the presence of a father further displaces the second woman, particularly if she is trying to play the father role. (Only one woman reported that she had consciously attempted to become a stepfather as opposed to a stepmother.)

That it was two women who were attempting to co-parent often caused more difficulty than lesbianism per se. As mentioned earlier, several women felt uncomfortable having another adult – especially a woman – watch them parent. Sharon described her response to Daphne's questions about some of the parental decisions Sharon made:

I'm struggling with getting rid of just all this crap that I've brought with me to age forty-two. And one of them is that, um, feeling very threatened when people question how I mother. Daphne questions a lot ... and um, it's tough when people start questioning. Men don't question your ability to mother. But other women do. Or at least some do. Certainly in a lesbian relationship where you've come with children and then all of a sudden there's questions being asked. It's very threatening ... I think you do feel more threatened when a woman asks the question. 'Cause that's the one area that men don't, you can dismiss them, you know, like you're not threatened by what they might offer. You can just kind of say, 'You don't know anything.'

The threat to maternal authority posed by another woman was often greater when she was also a biological mother. Each woman was unwilling to relinquish her monopoly on the authority over her children while at the same time resenting the same unwillingness in her partner. In the end, many of these couples ended up parenting more or less separately. Each biological mother looked after her own children, rendering 'cross-parenting' almost impossible. As Nanette described her situation:

Ellis's daughter is Ellis's daughter ... She's not my daughter, she's Ellis's daughter. And ultimately I can say and think whatever I wish, but Ellis handles the situation and deals with it.

Ellis revealed a similar lack of involvement in the lives of her partner's children:

I don't play any kind of a parent role in Nanette's kids' lives. Actually, we went through a time of trying [to co-parent], where I was more involved, but it didn't work so I backed out completely. I mean I don't even talk to them that much. And I'm going to have to deal with that in therapy.

It became apparent in the course of my interviews that although lesbianism is an issue that the blended family has to deal with, there are greater challenges. As Carol explained:

I don't think being lesbian makes a whole lot of difference in our lives. What makes a lot of difference is not having enough money and enough time, and being stressed out by, you know, having to work too many hours and that sort of thing. That's a whole lot more relevant to me – and I'm quite certain to all of us, including the cats – than [the fact] that Laura and I are both lesbian.

Whether the women were dealing with standard step-parenting issues or with ones that were unique to lesbian step-parenting, it became clear that this road to lesbian motherhood is a rocky one. It is not that it was always fights and struggles. Most of the women spoke of this time as one of tremendous emotional growth for all family members. They also found many rewards to life in a lesbian blended family, which is what kept them in their relationships. Nevertheless, the fact remains that becoming a lesbian mother in this context is no easy task.

In many repects, the task was simpler for the women who were already mothers. They had only to 'become' lesbian, whereas the previously childless women had to find a way to become mothers, and to do so with children who already had mothers and with partners who were not always willing to relinquish much of their mothering to others. Nonetheless, even though some of the previously childless women hesitated to refer to themselves as mothers, and some biological mothers were reluctant to share that label with their partners, the tasks these women performed constituted a kind of mothering. Having explored how the women in groups A and B *became* mothers, we are now in a position to turn our attention to what it meant to them to *be* mothers and to *do* mothering.

5

Mothering

When a heterosexual couple have children, they need not decide which partner will be the mother or dwell on what it means *to* mother. Although the actual content and style of the parenting done by women naturally varies from one individual to the next, we generally assume that the parenting that women do *is* mothering and examine our definition of mothering no further.

This is not the case with lesbian mothers, and especially with lesbian couples who are trying to mother together. The facile assumption that mothering is what the mother does is not applicable to lesbian couples. They *do* need to think about what a mother is and what she does. The reason for this is the presence of the non-biological mother. We think we know what a mother is, but what is a non-biological mother? What role does a second parenting woman play and what *is* she?

This chapter explores the responses that the women in my sample had to these questions. As in previous chapters, I use the term 'biological mother' to refer to those women who gave birth. Those women who did not give birth are called 'non-biological mothers.' The non-biological mother in a blended lesbian family is also called a 'stepmother' when discussed in relation to her partner's biological children. I use these terms for the sake of clarity only, because there is little consensus among lesbian families as to what the definitive terms might be.

NON-BIOLOGICAL MOTHERING

There are two ways in which women in my sample became non-biological mothers. Some became involved with women who had children from previous relationships, and some had babies with their lesbian partners through donor insemination. It became clear in the course of my research that there were important differences between being the biological mother and being the non-biological mother. These differences were more marked in the blended families than in the D.I. families.

I asked the stepmothers if they considered themselves 'the mother' or if there was another way in which they thought of themselves. Some women were reluctant to call themselves 'mother,' either because the child already had one and the presence of two mothers would be confusing or because there was a substantial difference between the role they played and that played by the biological mothers. Several women said they were the 'other parent,' a 'parental figure,' or an 'authority figure.' Carol saw herself as the 'parent' of Laura's children:

Whatever the hell that is ... I guess an adult who's responsible for their basic needs and also, um, doing what I can to see that they walk out into the world as emotionally equipped as possible.

In some instances, there were striking differences in the parenting roles the women played. Many stepmothers said that the biological mothers played a more 'primary' role, whereas the stepmothers played a more 'auxiliary' role. This usually meant that the biological mothers were more involved in the minutiae of their children's lives and in decision-making and matters of discipline. The role of the stepmother could involve anything from 'helping out' when necessary to playing a role very similar to that of the mother. Even in the latter case, however, there was still a certain primacy missing. Kim, the self-described 'other parent' of Evelyn's daughter, Anna, discussed the differences in the parenting roles that she and Evelyn played:

Evelyn does all the really personal type stuff with her. Um, like I guess it's a part of our different parenting styles too. Like Anna goes to Evelyn when she wants something, and she won't come to me because she knows I won't let her have it. Although we've both talked to her about sex and that kind of stuff, so it's not so much that. But I mean if Anna has a sore bum she talks to Evelyn about it. She doesn't talk to me. But I don't think it's that she couldn't talk to me. It's just that Evelyn's there and that's, she's always been around to talk to. Yeah, I think that's it. And Evelyn doesn't always realize too that, she doesn't think that the problems that Anna [and I have] have anything to do with me being a step-parent. She thinks it's my parenting style that pushes Anna away from me. But I don't think she realizes that I haven't had those first five years which are so important in bonding with a kid that, you know. I mean Evelyn's just got her, but I have to win her – win or lose her I mean.

Many of the stepmothers believed that one of the main differences between them and the biological mothers was their own relative lack of authority over the children. Some found that they had to watch that they did not overstep their boundaries. As Daphne explained:

There's still the biological bond, and that overrides a lot. And when the partner, you know, the partner may know a lot, but there's still that fine line that you don't cross ... It's been interesting for me because I've had to juggle just how much is my business and how much isn't.

For many stepmothers, the chief difficulty with not crossing the 'fine line' was that the line, at the biological mother's discretion, always seemed to be shifting. Many of the biological mothers in blended families found it difficult to 'sit back' and let another person assert authority over their children. Laura described what sometimes happened when Carol dealt with Laura's children:

I sometimes get defensive around stuff with the kids, and then suddenly Carol doesn't have authority where she thought she did, because I'm defensive or whatever. So it gets murky. We try to have equal authority.

Couples who had children through D.I. were much more likely to describe their two roles as the 'mother' and the 'other mother.' Having equal authority over the children was not a problem in these families, at least in the domestic realm. What was problematic was that the non-biological mothers had no *legal* authority. Several non-biological mothers reported difficulties in getting children admitted to hospital or in to see a doctor because they could not prove their maternal identity or their legal right to make medical decisions for the child. This legal barrier had emotional repercussions for the non-biological mothers, who could not help feeling excluded from their children's lives when in the public realm. Nancy spoke of trying to find day care for Astrid:

I went to four day cares in a week once looking for a day care for Astrid. And I had to explain that [she was not the birth mother] almost every time, partly because Elly had spoken to them first. And it's really hard, because I'm the weird one. Elly's the mom so she's not weird, but I'm the second one so I'm weird, like I'm the one that's the oddball. It's like maintaining my integrity and saying, 'It doesn't matter how they respond. I *am* Astrid's mom, and this is the way we've chosen. And it's great – it's the best way to parent as far as I'm concerned.' It comes down to how I'm going to react to their reaction, like if I get defensive and weird, then they're going to pick up on that and think it's weird and become defensive too. So I have to just be right there, like yeah, this is how we're parenting and it is different, but this is it – Astrid has two moms. So that was a big one. I had a big cry when I got home. And trying to get Elly to understand what that feels like, like why haven't I been the one phoning the day cares? Because I can't say that, yeah, I'm her mom without explaining I'm not her birth mom. I'm not her birth mom, and somehow that has to be there when you talk to a day care 'cause Elly is going to have to sign the papers and stuff. At least that's the way I see it all the time. I could probably go in there but it's like I want that to be clear – Astrid has two moms.

Although none of the non-biological D.I. mothers expressed this sentiment, many of the stepmothers believed that their lack of legal authority placed them in a very precarious position. The fact that they had not shared the birth and early upbringing of the children (which would have given them a more 'valid' claim to them), combined with their lack of legal status, created a very real danger that they could lose contact with the children should the relationship dissolve. According to Marda, 'women who are not biological parents are taking a big chance by becoming emotionally involved with children of their partners, because they have no rights whatsoever. None.'

Some stepmothers said that the main difference between them and the biological mothers had to do with the type and intensity of emotional involvement with the children. Janine, the biological mother of two teenagers, said that she was a 'parent figure' rather than a mother to Christine's son, Nicki. When I asked her what the difference was, she responded,

The first thing that comes to mind is worry. You know, I guess in some ways you don't have to worry quite as much as, you know, what's he going to be like when he grows up, where will he go to school, what do I want for him, what are my expectations for him, 'cause I leave that a lot to Christine. Not that I don't have any [worries], just that they're not as prominent as Christine's, I guess. Whereas I think when it's your own child, there's that bonding that comes with being biologically attached that is very very different. I think it would be different too if we had chosen to conceive Nicki in some fashion and he had grown up with us as our son legally, or whatever, from day zero. But the fact that he was somebody else's child, I mean this is a blended family. We can't fool ourselves and say, 'This is a natural family.' It's not. It's a blended family any way you look at it. And because of that, you know, I will not have a similar connection [to Nicki]. Not that it won't be as strong, but it won't be the same.

Even those stepmothers who felt as strong an emotional investment in the child as the biological mother acknowledged the existence of a special bond between the biological mothers and their children. Even some of the non-biological D.I. mothers conceded, sometimes reluctantly, that there was a different bond between a child and its biological mother. Denise described the bond between Bill and his biological mother, Wendy:

You know, it was amazing because I could tell no matter how good a time Bill and I were having together or how we were relating or the things I was showing him, all of a sudden there would be this look in Bill's eyes when he looked at his mom, you know, and I have never got that look from him. I have got some very close moments and times when he has made my heart melt, but Wendy's his mom, you know. I wouldn't have believed it, you know, because I equate myself to being an adoptive parent, and I don't think that any parent who has made a choice to adopt can be anything but a loving parent. It's a choice, you know. But there is a bond – a bio-bond – that you just can't break.

Some of the D.I. mothers rejected the idea of a 'bio-bond,' along with the closely related idea of 'maternal instinct.' Iris observed that after she gave birth to Steven, her partner Blaire seemed to be intimidated by what she assumed was Iris's newfound and innate maternal knowledge:

I think Blaire had some struggles with it at first because, again, it's what society says Blaire should be and what we think Blaire should be. And because there's an intimidation [factor] too, and this is, again, a society thing. I don't think that maternal instincts are that close to the surface, you know, and so I think there was [a sense] that I would know how to respond automatically because I had the baby, and Blaire wouldn't be able to respond because it's not her baby. And there was a couple of times where something would happen and I would say, 'Well, I think, you know, maybe we should do it this way or maybe we should do it that way. What do you think?' And then Blaire would feel intimidated because I knew that. But what she didn't know was that I read that [how to deal with the situation] in a book that she was too busy at school to read, that while I was home with the baby I read.

Some of the D.I. mothers believed that if the child responded differently to each mother, it was merely because one of them – usually the biological mother – spent more time with the child. Noreen, a biological D.I. mother, said:

There have been times where I think I can say things or ask them [children] to do things and they haven't listened, and Melanie will walk through the door [and they'll do it]. But that's pretty normal [with] the parent they don't see as much; that's pretty typical. I think if it was me out working all day [it would be the same]. Kids just react that way.

Marda, a stepmother, described a similar difference between her and the baby's biological mother:

Sue did spend more time with him because when she did work, she took him to work with her, um, when she wasn't working she was at home with him. So I wasn't there during the days. So he did spend a lot more time with her, and she spent a lot more time in a kind of nurturing role, just because she was there.

However, like all the stepmothers, Marda also believed that

children are probably always going to be bonded closer to their mothers. I think it's a rare thing if they're bonded closer to someone other than their biological mother. So although we were bonded together and he trusted me and he came to me all the time, and we did things together completely separate from Sue, I know his priority if he had to choose – he would still have chosen Sue over me.

Most of the D.I. mothers rejected this idea of a bond that could exist only between the biological mother and the child. Many claimed that there was no difference in the relationships they and their partners had with the children. Iris told me that she and Blaire were working to minimize the differences between 'biological mother' and 'non-biological mother.' She described those differences as follows:

Well, a lot of them are societally imposed, where people don't automatically call Blaire 'mother' or don't automatically assume that Blaire, you know, changes the diapers or feeds him and stuff like that. Maybe even they assume that she takes on the father role, you know. So those types of impositions we try to diminish a lot ... We're a parental unit and we're not divided by those distinctions, biological and non-biological.

Some of the non-biological mothers felt they had to establish with the child a bond that they assumed came more easily to the biological mother because she had given birth. Yet, in establishing that bond, they also became a mother. As Nancy explained:

I'm not her [Astrid's] birth mother, but I'm her mother. I think that more and more that's starting to [become evident]. Like for a while, especially after she was born and stuff, it was like I needed the time that Elly had carried her in her womb ... She was there with Elly for all that time, and so when she first came out it was like now I needed to have that time. And so our relationship keeps growing now, you know, like as she gets bigger and we do [things together]. Yeah, I'm Astrid's mom. I really am now, you know. We're equals in a lot of ways, Elly and I now. Like last night Astrid had a nightmare and she didn't want to be with Elly, she wanted to be with me. She'll go back and forth that way, like whoever suits her need more.

Each of the non-biological D.I. mothers considered herself the 'other mother,' and said that if there were any difference between her parenting tasks and those of the biological mother, it was only that the biological mother breastfed and she did not. Other differences were attributed to variation in parenting styles. Each mother was equally primary to the child, and the couples often took pains not to exclude each other in any way. Iris described the importance of language with respect to the latter:

Blaire and I are both very careful to phrase everything properly. We always say it's 'our' son because we're both so sensitive – it makes me sick – that if one of us said, 'It's my son' the other one would go, 'It's my son too.' So we're very careful in how we word things, so that we include each other all the time that way.

The D.I. mothers divided parenting duties between them as equally as possible. Frequently, the partners would alternate part-time shifts or seasonal jobs, not only so that each had equal time with the baby but also so that the child did not have to enter day care at too young an age.

One of the biggest problems facing the D.I. couples was deciding what the children would call them. They shared parenting equally, each woman considering herself a mother. What they needed were names that would reflect the importance and equality of each woman's bond to the child yet also differentiate the women for purposes of identification. Several women were uncomfortable with the idea of one partner being called 'mom' and the other being called by her first name. Some couples resolved this dilemma by referring to themselves only by their first names, and by asking friends and family to cooperate in this endeavour.

For those women who came to believe that a child *should* have someone to call 'mom,' the challenge was to find a name for the non-biological mother. Elly described the difficulties she and Nancy had meeting this challenge:

When Astrid was first born we made a joke that Nancy was the momma and I was the mooma because I was nursing. So for a long time we would be momma and mooma, and that was funny. We both call ourselves Astrid's mother ... She [Nancy] struggles with how she should identify herself with this child. Because if she says she's the mother, she gets asked 'how was the labour?' and 'are you still nursing?' sorts of questions. And that's hard, so sometimes she says 'co-parent' and sometimes she says 'mother,' and I think that's hard for her. But to everyone else, if we're ever saying anything to people that we're out to, we say both mothers. At work I'm not out, and so Nancy is my room-mate and she babysits Astrid.

Denise related a similar struggle:

We tried to work on another term for me, something – 'mother' in another language – that works well with English. Well, that doesn't work. We haven't found anything. And then I don't want him to just call me Denise. That's not special. I don't think that that is special enough. So right now when I talk to him now I call myself D.D. But the problem is that we're planning a second child, and I'm going to be that second child's bio-mother. So how do we have D.D. and W.W. [this works better with her real initials] and mom and mom? We haven't found a solution to that one yet. I don't know. I'm hoping Bill will help us with the solution. He's a very bright child – he's brilliant actually – so we're figuring that Bill will help us with it too. .

Several women said that if both partners were called 'mom,' they would each become a generic maternal entity, playing a role but having no individual identity. Others worried about ramifications in the public world. Denise described one possible scenario:

You know, it's one thing for me to be open and courageous to the cashier at Food-for-Less [if the cashier were to ask who the mother is, which had happened] when I want to be. But what about the day Bill walks up, and we're in the cashier's line and he looks at me and goes, 'mommy,' and he looks at Wendy and goes, 'mom,' and the cashier goes [looks confused]? You know, I don't have control of that situation, then, because Bill had control of the terms, right, so I don't. It's definitely an issue, and I don't have the solution for it.

Determining names was no easy struggle for the D.I. couples. In the end, two of the couples decided that the child would call the biological mother 'mom' and the other mother by her first name. One couple referred to themselves by their first names. For the other couples, the question remained unanswered. Like Denise, they hoped that the child would discover terms that were the most comfortable for him or her.

Names were not an issue for the blended families. The biological mother was generally called 'mom' while the non-biological mother was usually referred to by name. There were, however, particular challenges that the stepmothers had to face. As discussed earlier, the sharing of parental authority was a major issue in these families. Interestingly, when I asked the stepmothers if they shared authority equally with the biological mothers, the answer was almost always 'yes and no':

Basically, nobody has any authority over Sandy [teenager]. And, um, it's been said to Charlene [six-year-old] that if [I] Andrea tells you to do something or asks you to do something, or whatever, then you're expected to do it. Um, but she generally doesn't respond as quickly to me as she does to her mom.

When it comes to things like, Dan likes to jack off in school ... when it comes to things like the bottom line on what's going to happen around that, the last decision is usually Laura's [biological mother]. We've usually at least talked about it. She may do what I think is the most appropriate. Often at least part of it. I see myself as being more authoritative with the kids and Laura being much more permissive. I would tend to be harder on him. Um, we squabble about that every once in a while. But when it comes to things like doing something at home, Dan will tend to come to me and ask if there's something, or I will be the one to tell them that they need to do something. I think in that way the balance is a little more in my direction. So I guess it's pretty equal, but it's different at the same time.

Women who were biological mothers to their own children and stepmothers to their partner's children found that trying to co-mother, or even just mother in tandem with another woman, required a change in some of the mothering they did. As Ellis explained:

In terms of my kids I would be quite different outside the relationship than I am in the relationship in some senses ... You know, my expectations of Rhonda [her biological daughter] would be quite different ... Nanette has fairly rigid kinds of rules, like she wants the house quiet by ten o'clock. And until last summer Rhonda's bedroom was next to ours, and she used to drive Nanette crazy because Rhonda tends to be a late-night person and Nanette had the expectation that she would settle down and be quiet by ten at night. Well, I conformed to that because I knew it was really important to Nanette, but I knew it wouldn't be the way that I would operate. You know, so there's things like that, things that are important to Nanette. And I mean that goes both ways, because there's things that have changed with her kids because they're important to me ... You know, she would be quite different with her kids if I wasn't there too. That's the reality of a relationship. I think you, the whole system changes because you're trying to create a new system.

Many of the women, in both D.I. families and blended families, said that mothering completely changed the focus of the relationship they had with their partners. Elly elaborated:

The focus of the relationship is rearing our child and I don't even remember what that focus was before then. It's so, it sort of sweeps everything else away. You know, I think that will change as Astrid gets older and is more independent, but right now our world [revolves] around getting her up, getting her fed, getting her this, getting her that. She goes to bed, we have half an hour of exhausted talk, and we fall together in bed exhausted. Our focus is on her. It has to be with young children, it just is. And I think that will change, and I don't know what we'll discover our relationship to be when she's four or five. It's changed a lot, and a lot of that is really neat and cooperative. We share a lot of stuff together and we cooperate in zillions of ways. Like I think Astrid is probably more co-parented than just about any other kid in the world. She's spent equal time with each of us. We equally do everything with her, like in terms of sharing responsibilities. The only thing that's different is I'm still nursing. So there's that cooperation, that mutual effort to survive that's there.

Whether the two women in a lesbian family equally shared the parenting or became 'mom' and 'other adult,' both had to think about what it meant to be a mother. Because the non-biological mothers were working to establish themselves as some sort of 'mother,' they needed to determine what a mother is. Similarly, the biological mothers, faced with the necessity of sharing mothering, had to become much more aware of what it means to be a mother.

BEING A MOTHER

Being a mother and doing mothering are closely linked but not synonymous. When I asked the women what it meant to be a mother, some gave me a list of the things they do as a mother. It appears, however, that being a person who performs mothering tasks is only part of what a mother is. Several women answered the question by describing what they 'got out of' mothering, for example, a feeling of pride for doing a good job raising children or a sense of stability and family. '[Motherhood] keeps me on the straight and narrow and not going wacky,' Trish said. She added:

Another thing that being a mother does for me is when I do things for my kids, you know, how happy they are and how wonderful they think it is and, you know, like 'right on,' that sort of thing ... And my kids are proud of me [for going to school], and that [also] makes me feel good.

Several women believed that being a lesbian mother means being a mother *and* a father in the sense that all parenting tasks are performed by the mothers, even ones, such as disciplining, that might often be performed by fathers in heterosexual families. Additionally, it is women who undertake household, yard, and car maintenance. Thus the children are seeing women play roles that tend, in heterosexual families, to be distributed along gender lines.

Some women said that being a mother means that their children become their top priority. Trish said:

My one priority is to my children. And it's not just love there. That's the other thing about being a mother. It's not just love. It's like I have a responsibility to them.

Similarly, Christine revealed that her son, Nicki, had initially been her 'sole project.' Over time, however, her attitude toward her 'project' changed:

I don't have as strong an investment in being the best parent possible – like I did when Nicki was my project – in the sense that when I had him I hadn't completed anything at that point; or I had been taught to believe I hadn't completed anything and I was pretty worthless, and that sort of business. So he was going to be my opportunity to indicate [my worth], and he became my life and breath and soul. You can't do that, you know, you end up exhausted and disillusioned. And now I can freely admit that there's days I wish I'd never had him.

Many women said that being a mother means being willing to perform endless tasks and to take on an extremely challenging, emotionally rewarding, but more or less thankless role. Several said that being a mother means being a kind of friend. Evelyn, for example, saw mothering as a biological imperative and friendship as something she had to work towards:

I think Anna [daughter] feels more like a friend to me, and that's what I've always wanted. Like when I had a child I wanted, it was more important for me to be a friend than to be a mother. I don't care if I'm a mother or not. That comes naturally. That's a bonus. And Kim [partner] really disagreed with that. She really thought that was wrong. I should be a parent with the child. But [I believe] my life will have been successful if we're friends. That's more important.

For Evelyn, being a friend meant being less authoritarian than a mother.

Some respondents stated that being a mother means contributing a well-balanced person to the next generation and a piece of themselves to future generations. When I asked Rose what it meant to her to be a mother, she said, 'I think to be able to share my love with a child, to bring a child into the world for future generations. I guess a legacy to the world, an extension of myself.'

One of the most striking responses was that being a mother means having an adult role. Considering that the usual adult roles for women are 'wife' and 'mother,' we can see why this issue might be so important to the women in my sample, who are, for the most part, excluded from these roles. Lesbian couples are generally not perceived either by their families or by society as 'married,' and therefore attached lesbian women are usually not seen as 'wives.' Men tend to be seen as adult when they become financially independent; their central roles revolve around their careers and their status as breadwinners. Although lesbian women have to be their own breadwinners, it is not financial independence but rather motherhood that often identifies women as 'adult' in our society. Motherhood appears to be one of few acceptable routes to an adult identity to which a lesbian woman has access. This may rarely be a reason to have a child, but it certainly seems to be a part of what it means to lesbian women to be a mother.

WHAT A MOTHER DOES

As discussed earlier, being a mother and carrying out mothering tasks are closely related. All the women were able to articulate what it meant *to* mother. The overwhelming majority said that a mother's primary task was to nurture the children. In explaining her response, Nanette differentiated between 'mothering' and 'parenting':

The mothering part to me means that I consciously nurture. I am consciously aware that the need for nurturing is required by children [if they are] to grow and develop as whole human beings. To *parent* you don't have to nurture. You can provide food, clothing, shelter, and you can be called a parent. But to be called a father or a mother or to be called a mother, then you have to be willing to get in there, down and dirty emotionally, down and dirty – *real*. You have to be there through thick and thin. And you have to answer them when they cry. And you have to get up off your duff and walk into their room and pick them up. Because I don't believe [that it's possible to spoil a child]. I do believe they can manipulate you after a period of time, but I don't believe in spoiling. And if they're crying, there's a need and that has to be met. And if they're sad or depressed or they're slamming doors, there's a need and I have to be there, and I have to get off my duff and shut off the television or close my book. And that's mothering to me. That's not parenting. That's mothering. I guess that's being there emotionally for the kids.

Many other women agreed that mothering means being emotionally involved with, and available to, the children. Other important aspects of mothering that the respondents cited were 'loving,' 'holding,' 'supporting,' 'taking pride in,' 'exploring and learning with,' and 'teaching.' Like Nanette, many of the women felt that mothering means unconditionally meeting the children's needs, whatever those needs might be. Kim explained:

She's [baby] totally dependent on me, and [being a mother means] being able to give her what she needs. And being that person who will do that for her no matter what. You know, I mean if she's cranky and crying she still has to have it done. I guess as she gets older it'll be sharing, and I want to do fun stuff together and enjoy each other's company.

Most of the respondents echoed Kim's observation that mothering changes as the children grow and develop. Sharon described the primary task of mothering at one particular stage in her children's development:

I'm in transition ... my relationships with the kids are in transition because they are becoming adults. So right now it [mothering] means – well, the next stages are launching their independence, you know, like financially. And I think Kandy is doing pretty well emotionally. That was speeded up a little bit, I think, by Daphne and I getting together. And financially is another one ... so right now mothering is kind of pushing them out, pushing them away.

For all the women, mothering denotes some combination of the various tasks, discussed earlier. Two women in the sample summed up the job of mothering as follows:

It brings a line from the book *Murmel Murmel Murmel*. The little girl is looking for somebody to take the baby she found in the hole in the sandbox, and she talks to all these different people and one says 'Well, what can I do with it?' And the little girl says, 'Well, it's for loving and hugging and kissing and burping.' It's for taking care of. It's for nurturing. You nurture a baby and give them what they need and answer questions, and you create safe places and you just grow up with them, you know. I think, with babies, mothering is being there in whatever [way] they need at the time. It's for creating guidelines and, you know, describing the world until they can do it on their own. I think it's ever changing as their needs change and you go with them.

Nurturing, I think, is a very important part of motherhood, nurturing and caring and loving, giving, sharing, teaching. All of that is what makes a mother. That's why it's easy for us to make no distinctions between the two of us [mothers] because we both do that so well with him [baby].

The idea that 'we both do [motherhood] so well' is significant. If we consider what these women say it means to be a mother and to do mothering, we can see that anyone – male or female, biologically attached to the child or not – could *be* a mother and anyone could *do* mothering. Why is it, then, that some respondents who perform these tasks feel uncomfortable calling themselves 'mother'? Why is it that some biological mothers will not allow the women who share mothering tasks with them to share the label 'mother'? As we have seen, part of the reason is that the women need labels to differentiate themselves. But this is more than a matter of convention or semantic convenience; it is a matter of what might be called the 'mothers' culture.'

THE INNER CIRCLE

A point that came up in every interview I had with D.I. mothers (both biological and non-biological) was their discomfort with outsiders' questions about the child. Questions like 'Is his father's hair that colour?' are impossible to answer when one was impregnated with the sperm of an unknown donor. Answering such questions honestly requires one to 'come out' to complete strangers (at least to the extent of admitting the use of artificial insemination). Some questions posed to the women in my sample were even more personal: 'How was the labour?' 'Did you have an episiotomy?' 'Are you still breastfeeding?' At first, I was shocked that people would presume to ask such questions of anyone. But in discussing the matter (especially with heterosexual mothers of my acquaintance), I realized that these are the sorts of things that mothers feel they have a licence to discuss with each other.

It is possible that heterosexual biological mothers are not as struck by such discourse as are those women who are, to some extent, excluded from it because they are lesbian or because they are non-biological mothers. Wendy described her experience:

Oh, it's amazing what people [will ask]. It's like opening a door to your soul when you have a child. And the thing is that it almost becomes a reality too, because I've found that things that I was inhibited about before the birth certainly didn't bother me afterwards. Like I [had] thought, 'I'm never going to breastfeed in public,' but that kind of stuff all goes away. And so you do become an open soul to a certain degree and lose a lot of your inhibitions. And I found [that] those questions come more from women and more from mothers who all of a sudden are relating to that, you know. It's like you have this inner circle, and they can ask you just about anything.

Similarly, Blaire commented:

You sort of enter this 'mommy' world, you know, and that's a whole other world. And you realize what you have in common with straight women – you have motherhood in common. But somehow that denies some of your lesbianism, so it's sort of a conditional relationship.

'Inner circle,' 'mommy world,' and 'mommy's club' are among the terms used to refer to the same thing. What is being described here might be called the *culture of motherhood*, a subculture with its own language and initiation criteria. Wendy offered her understanding of it:

It's definitely part of networking, I think. But I think it's also [that] the child is so much a part of you. Before you were a person, you know, and now you're a mother, and so you are this being with the child attached to you that you know very well ... Like staying up with it all night or changing their poopy diapers or whatever. These are not just things that you do casually. These are things that you do, like [if it was] anything else in your life, it would be considered intense. If you made love that much, for instance, it would be considered intense, you know. So it's something that becomes a real part of you. And yeah, you share it with people, and I think women have to. Mothers have to do that.

Elly shared her perceptions:

It's women's culture ... and it's really nice. We sit down, and you can ask a woman – if you're sitting there with a brand-new baby – you can ask her how her labour was, and she'll tell you, and you sit and talk and share. It's our culture we share. It's really great. It's just we [lesbians] screw up the whole system, like we throw in all these twists that make it really difficult to deal with. But I mean I didn't know about that culture until I walked around pregnant. Women smile at you, talk about, you know, 'Is it your first?' 'Do you want a boy or a girl?' – like out of the blue. It becomes women's – it's women's public domain.

Many interviewees reported that having given birth is one of the entrance requirements to this 'club,' which to some extent excludes adoptive mothers and non-biological mothers. (Some women even sensed in other mothers resentment towards women who are not biological mothers). As Denise put it, 'If you have had one [a baby], it's an experience that no one can be a part of, and no one can understand unless you have personally done it.' Wendy added:

I know that Denise felt particularly out of place, and I got this impression from some of the women that it's like 'well, you've never had a child so what would you know?' kind of attitude. Not all women, but a lot of women get really righteous after they've gone through that, had a baby.

The foregoing supports the idea that maternal authority is the only legitimate claim to authority that women have traditionally been allowed in Western society. (By 'authority' in this context I mean both knowledge and power.) If this observation is true, it would explain why women guard this authority so closely. As we saw earlier, biological mothers who have not shared mothering from birth with another woman have varying degrees of difficulty relinquishing any of their authority to their female partner. Daphne, a non-biological mother in a blended family, expressed sentiments that were shared by all the step-mothers:

Sometimes I feel left out. And sometimes it's just like being a kid and you're in the middle of it. Because Sharon is a mother, she goes into mother mode and I, I find that interesting. You know, you watch people that are mothers, and they have this 'I know it all' approach. I watch with Laura and Carol [step-parenting friends], you know, and Laura knows it all and Carol and the kids know nothing. And I said one day, 'I often wonder just because someone biologically gives birth to a child, why all of a sudden it makes them the most knowledgeable person on everything under the sun, and the rest of us, until we give birth, don't really know anything.'

Motherhood is *the* common female experience, connecting women across historical, cultural, and geographic space. It is women's unique realm of authority and power. Moreover, this authority would seem to be founded in a special *maternal epistemology*. This epistemology is neither innate nor unchanging, since the social experiences and meanings of motherhood do change across time, culture, and geography. It can begin with the physiological act of giving birth (regardless of ceremony, ritual, or meaning attached to it) that all biological mothers have in common. The role they play in the cycle of life does give them a kind of knowledge no other person can have, but this knowledge alone does not constitute an epistemology.

Mothering as giving birth can be linked with mothering as behaviour. Experiences of mothering and the children themselves are *owned* by mothers and mothers alone. Certainly, in many times and places, men have had legal ownership of both women and their offspring, but this is not the same as the possession one has of something that is born of one's body.[1] The experience of giving birth and the social role of mothering place women in particular social spaces inhabited mainly by other mothers. Maternal epistemology springs from these spaces, the concepts of which are the foundations of maternal discourse. By sharing the details of birth and mothering, women weave and reweave the connections between themselves, not only in the present but also in the past and in the future.[2]

Although it appears that mothers occupy a particular cultural space with its own entrance requirements, discourse, and epistemology, the content and perimeters of such a culture remain largely unknown. It would be naive, however, to assume that there is just one culture of motherhood. Motherhood does not even have a common biological basis (women can be non-biological mothers). Thus there is no common physiological experience of motherhood, and there cannot be said to be a common emotional experience of it. There might be broad commonalities to the social experiences of mothering in Canada, but it seems likely that experiences would vary according to location, ethnicity, religion, socio-economic class, and cultural tradition. The culture of motherhood might, in fact, be composed of several subcultures of motherhood having varying degrees of interpenetration.

Nonetheless, it appears that part of what it means to *be* a mother is to be *recognized* as a mother. And this recognition can only come from others – in particular, other mothers. We have seen that the women in my sample who had not given birth were less welcome in the maternal discourse than those who had, and we have seen that non-biological mothers in blended lesbian families are rarely allowed a real claim to

1 I do not necessarily mean long-term or constant possession. Some women give their children up for adoption. Other women's children are taken from them. Some women abuse or even kill their children. Many women hire others (e.g., nannies and day-care providers) to perform 'mothering' tasks. This does not negate the fact that the feeling of possession one has of something that is born of one's body is different from any other feeling of possession of any other thing or person.

2 Ruddick's (1983) idea of 'maternal thinking' is relevant here. Ruddick argues that the 'agents of maternal practice, acting in response to the demands of their children, acquire a conceptual scheme – a vocabulary and logic of connections – through which they order and express the facts and values of their practice' (214). Maternal thinking is thus 'a unity of reflection, judgement, and emotion' arising from the biological, emotional, intellectual, psychological, spiritual, moral, and social requirements of mothering and conditions under which mothering is performed (214). Maternal thinking can thus be seen as a foundation of maternal epistemology, a key component of what I describe as a 'culture of motherhood.'

maternal authority. I doubt that birth is the primary criterion here. Rather, an important criterion is labour. Mothering is a job – it is labour. The labour that accompanies birth is only the beginning. Among women with young babies, however, this birthing labour constitutes a large part of the labour they have performed so far. Thus a woman who has not given birth has missed a significant proportion of the labour of mothering.

I suspect that as time goes on and the children get older, it matters less and less if a woman actually gave birth to a child, as long as she has raised the child since birth. But the second woman in a blended lesbian family has done none of the labouring involved in mothering. Because she has done none of the labouring, she has not earned the title of 'mother' and all that goes with it. Implied in the term 'mother' is the possession of 'maternal authority.' Once a woman is recognized as a 'mother,' as a being possessing this authority, she becomes a participant in the maternal discourse; she is a member of the inner circle – the culture of motherhood.

A woman's lesbianism can marginalize her within the maternal discourse because here, as in most social spheres in Canada, there is an assumption of heterosexuality. To enter the discourse and offer information about herself and her life, a lesbian woman has to 'come out' of a stigmatized closet. Although lesbianism does not exclude women from the discourse, it sometimes makes interaction there awkward. Those aspects of mothering that are unique to lesbian women have not been acknowledged in the mainstream, heterosexual maternal discourse. There, as elsewhere, lesbian women are rendered invisible by the assumption of universal heterosexuality.

Lesbian D.I. couples also present a substantial challenge to established maternal culture by demanding that they (both partners) not be differentiated on the basis of having given birth or not. By insisting that non-biological mothers are mothers too, these women have the potential to alter the understanding mothers have of motherhood. In this sense, lesbian motherhood through donor insemination can be seen as a revolutionary activity.

It is those aspects of mothering that are unique to lesbian women that give life in a lesbian family some of *its* distinctiveness. As the next chapter demonstrates, there are particular characteristics of lesbian families and particular challenges that usually only lesbian families have to face.

6

Lesbian Families

There are characteristics that are unique to lesbian families, and there are issues that only lesbian (and probably sometimes gay male) families have to face. This chapter begins with an exploration of the process whereby lesbian couples come to identify themselves, and be identified by others, as 'families.' The discussion continues with an examination of what it is like to live in a lesbian family.

Each D.I. couple reported that the addition of a child changed how they perceived themselves. They were no longer a couple – they were a family. For Tina and her partner, this transition occurred almost immediately after the birth of the child:

It was an instant sense of family. It was like before it had been Rose and me, and the baby was an unknown quantity. We had no idea what he was going to look like. We didn't know what the father looked like ... [When the baby was born] it was just instant family. There was instant bonding.

Iris was among the women who echoed this sentiment:

Now we're a family. We have, we're a family of five now instead of a family of four, including the [two] animals, of course. Now we're different. I mean Blaire's and my relationship isn't different. We still treat each other the same way, with the same respect, but now we have a little person around too who makes us a family.

Blaire described what was involved in the transition from couple to family:

It's, um, it's not like something new that we don't know, but it *is* something new that we don't know. I mean we're learning all the time how we have to change how we relate to each other, how we have to know that not only now do we just talk about caring for Steven – what did he have for lunch today, you know, all those sorts of daily things – to talking about our feelings about each other, what we're doing for each other, what we're doing for ourselves, and how we can't do what we used to do as much, or not at all, um, our expectations for each other, our changing and need to change and being able to give up things that we could do before willingly and, I don't know, regretfully, to mourn them for a minute and then say, 'Okay, we can't do them any more, but it doesn't mean we won't be doing them again.' You know, Iris's new favourite word is 'family.' She comes in the door and it's 'hello, family.' You know, it's changed everything, you know, and, we don't resist the change too much, but we can't predict it and so we sort of learn it as it comes along.

Although most of the women experienced an 'instant bond' with the baby, the transition to 'family' was not always so immediate. Elly described the process she and Nancy went through:

I don't think it [having the baby] did [immediately transform us into a family], although I wanted it to and it has now. I think it took a long time for that to take, and I think that's because we struggled with a lot of issues surrounding whose baby is it, you know ... Like just all that stuff [ideas about what a 'real' family is] came and it's all there and it's internalized within us and so it, I mean we wanted it to be, and in my head, I mean it was partly that way. It was partly a family, but I don't think it was at the beginning. I think it is now. I really feel like we're a family now. We're definitely not a couple, and that's from sharing the responsibilities of having a child for a year and a half has made us into a family, but I don't think we automatically were.

Feeling like a family is one thing – being perceived as such is sometimes quite another. As Elly's experiences demonstrate, people's reluctance or inability to acknowledge a lesbian couple and their children as a family can make it difficult for the couple to see themselves as one. For friends, family, and acquaintances who have not accepted that the couple are unequivocally a couple (which can be seen as a type of family itself), it can be difficult to acknowledge that the 'couple' are now a childed family. The biological mother's parents are often able and willing to accept the child as their grandchild, but they sometimes hesitate to acknowledge that the partner has any relationship to them, their daughter, or their grandchild. Many women found that their close friends and members of the lesbian community were most likely to acknowledge their family status. Blaire described how perceptions varied depending on the source:

Well, in the [lesbian] community definitely we're perceived as a family. Iris's family perceives us as a family. My family is learning how to perceive us as a family. You know, just because we're lesbians they have some difficulty. They can't see us as a heterosexual family, so there's some resistance ... Anybody who knows us as a family treats us as a family.

As we shall see later, many of the challenges lesbian families face can be traced to the lack of social acknowledgment that they are families.

The process of becoming families and coming to perceive themselves as such was different for the blended families in that the biological mothers tended to feel that they and their children already constituted families. Thus the transition was generally not that of *becoming* a family – it was *changing* from one kind of family to another. Like the D.I. families, the blended families found that a lesbian family was not widely acknowledged or supported except by close friends and sometimes by family members. However, some women did find that people's perceptions changed. Laura, the biological mother in a blended family, described how perceptions of her personal status changed once she regained custody of her children:

Actually, when I was just with a partner, people saw me as single. Even those members of my family who I was most out with and who were most comfortable would tend to see me as a single person ... and I probably saw myself that way anyhow. But with kids, yeah, I'm a family, we're a unit ... and I'm not single. But my guess is my family would see me as a single person with a lover if it weren't for the kids. They do tend to view us as a family unit with the kids.

Many of the stepmothers in blended families faced the same problem outside the home that they did inside: they were not acknowledged as mothers. If people (including the biological mother) are unwilling to give the stepmother a parental role or label, it is difficult for them to see the group as a family; instead, they see a mother, her children, and her lover. This tendency became even more evident when I asked the respondents to identify the people that they believed constituted their families. Women in blended families sometimes said that their families consisted of their partners and their own biological children. Ellis was among the stepmothers who excluded their partners' children from their conception of the family unit:

I would see Nanette and my kids as being my family. And at this point I don't include her kids in that. That actually is a real area of tension for us, um, I find her kids really difficult to deal with.

This was not always the case, however, and some stepmothers – always ones with no biological children of their own – found it much easier to feel that their partners' children were family to them.

Some of the women in blended families made a conscious effort not to label themselves as a 'family.' Nanette explained that she, her children, Ellis, and Ellis's daughter actually composed three families. She and Ellis were one family, she and her children the second, and Ellis and Ellis's daughter were the third. She explained how this arrangement was to everyone's advantage:

We don't presume that we are a family. And I think that has created a closer, ah, an opportunity for closeness that would not have been there if I had just assumed that we were a family and dammit behave like one! Because it gives choice. You know there's always a choice. She can choose to share with me or she can choose not to, and there's no hurt feelings, you know, there's no assumption. And vice versa.

In contrast, the D.I. mothers, whether biological or non-biological, always included their partners and their children in their conception of 'family.'

Another unique aspect of lesbian family life was revealed when I asked the respondents to identify the members of their extended families. Almost all the women in both the D.I. and blended families said that their friends were their extended family. Although consanguineous family members such as parents or (more frequently) siblings were sometimes included, they were almost always secondary. For most women, the primary and most actively involved extended families were composed of friends, both homosexual and heterosexual.

SUPPORT NETWORKS

Although emotional and material support was generally more forthcoming from friends than from relatives, it should be noted that many of the women in the sample lived some distance from their parents and siblings. Very few had relatives in Alberta. (This is not merely a coincidence; often the friction between lesbian women and their families is an impetus for the former to move away.) Some women did believe, however, that their parents and siblings would be more involved in their newly formed families if they were geographically closer.

As mentioned in an earlier chapter, the parents of the biological mothers often considered themselves grandparents and more or less behaved as such, by providing emotional and material support. It was not uncommon, for example, for the biological mother's parents to purchase the crib or clothing for the baby. Very often the grandparents restricted their interest to their grandchild, largely ignoring their daughter's other 'family.'

Some grandparents were discomforted less by the fact that their daughter was part of a lesbian couple than by the fact that the child would be 'illegitimate.' The parents of both biological and non-biological mothers expressed this concern. Noreen recalled:

My mom's concern was that these children were not going to have a name. And I think [it's] the same kind of thing as having children out of wedlock for her. Like in her time that was not done, you know, and so that was more the stigma that she was dealing with.

Sometimes the stigma of having an 'illegitimate' grandchild put even more emotional distance between the woman and her parents. This was especially true for the biological mothers. Yet the reverse was sometimes true for the parents of the non-biological mothers. Because it was not *their* illegitimate grandchild, they were more likely to be involved with him or her than had their own daughter given birth to it. Tina described her father's attitude towards her non-biological son, Tim:

My sister once said that she was jealous and hurt because my father treated Tim better [than the sister's illegitimate children]. And it's because of that distance. It's not a bloodline; it's not illegitimate in *his* family. Whereas my sister has given birth to illegitimate children – that's his problem.

Because the women in the blended families had, for the most part, much older children, their relatives were not called upon for the same sorts of assistance often requested by parents of babies. And, because the children were older and had been born into a heterosexual relationship, the parents of the biological mothers had a history of being grandparents to them. Thus they did not have to struggle with becoming grandparents under unusual circumstances. It was, however, extremely unlikely that a stepmother's parents would regard some other woman's children as their grandchildren.

A few of the couples, from both D.I. and blended families, said that they received no support from their relatives. Many more women in the two sample groups said that, although they received a degree of acknowledgment or emotional support from their parents, they received very little material support from them. As Noreen explained:

You know, basically we did it on our own, and I think that's how we've done it all along pretty well. You know, it's always nice if you get something from somewhere, but basically you know you're going to do it on your own ... Of course, when you don't have the big marriage where you get all the gifts, you know, that's always a good start for some people.

Kim expressed a similar sentiment:

I think lesbian couples do more of it for themselves. I mean look at, nobody gets wedding presents ... Like how do heterosexual couples start? ... I mean anniversaries – my parents buy all my brothers and sisters anniversary presents. They don't even recognize that we might have one.

I do not want to give the impression that these women spent their time moping about the presents lesbian women never receive. I specifically asked them to comment on the types of *material* support they received. When I did not make this specification, and just asked them about the 'support' they received, they always talked about emotional support. The material aspect of the support was something I had to draw out.

Some women felt that their relatives offered support because it was proper and not necessarily because they had warm feelings for the lesbian family. Evelyn said that her relatives and Kim's relatives 'went through the motions. They know the motions to go through [when someone has a baby].' Kim believed that because her sister Sally had a baby shortly before she did, her parents were obligated to treat Evelyn and Kim better than they might have otherwise. As she explained:

In our family, like fair is fair. You know: we spend fifteen dollars on your birthday present, so we've got to spend fifteen on everyone else's. So whatever they do for Sally, they have to do for me kind of thing. So it's kind of nice in a way ... Whereas if it was just me, they might be able to get away with not doing certain things that we would normally do for a person in that situation, you know.

Many of the women in the overall sample found that their siblings were far more enthusiastic and involved than their parents. Nancy described relations with her siblings:

They [brothers] are really great, and my sister is a little bit more – she's not as willing to accept that we're actually lesbians. But that we can have a really great relationship together and stuff is okay with her, and that we're raising a kid together, that's fine. She can see Astrid as pretty close to like a niece, but I don't know if she's quite made that connection. It's pretty good with my siblings. They were great when we were there [visiting] and stuff.

As mentioned earlier, the greatest amount of support, acknowledgment, and assistance generally came from friends, who as a result were often considered closer members of the families than were relatives. Lesbian friends did not always start out with an understanding of why these couples wanted to have children, but with a little education, they usually came around. Each couple had a circle of friends, both lesbian and heterosexual, who offered enthusiastic support through the entire family-making process. Tina noted how important friends can be:

In our case both our families live some distance away, so we're not in regular contact with them. So really our circle of friends is the immediate family in that respect. And they probably are more important in our lives than if we were a heterosexual couple, because your whole lifestyle is, um, under attack – that's too strong a term – but is in question from the rest of society. [Whereas] everything you do as a heterosexual couple – as long as you don't put on a rubber suit and run around the neighbourhood – is fine. There's no question that almost everything you do, because you are a lesbian, is called into question. So yeah, I think you're always looking to be, you know, bolstered by people who have the same kind of lifestyle or the same values that you do.

The support network described by Elly was fairly typical of many of the families:

I think I get as much support from my family as I would if I was in a heterosexual relationship. I get quite a bit. I mean my mom bought the crib, which is sort of the classic grandmother thing to do. And I had a house full of baby clothes before Astrid was even born from my sister and my sister-in-law, my mom. I guess I get half as much as I would if Nancy's family was as supportive as well. I try to imagine what that would be like – that would be Christmas, it would be great. So we don't get any support from her side of the family, so that's different, I guess, than it would be. I don't, I don't feel I get nearly the same amount of support from the community at large, like the people at work that I'm out to … They don't understand my family. They somehow think I'm a single parent, but I have this friend, you know. Like it's confusing to them so they don't have a box to put me in, so I don't think I get as much support from them. But my close lesbian community [friends] I get quite a bit of support from. I had two years of diaper service paid for from all our friends, which is extraordinary. It's a large amount of money. It's like $1800 for two years of diaper service. People went together and paid for it. And I've had, I mean I happen to have a couple of more well-off friends and that, I mean they've bought tons of things for Astrid. Single lesbians without children, you know. Astrid loves them; they bring goodies all the time. So I have that, but that's sort of financial and some forms of other support but I don't … I don't feel like I have the support of any kind of community as much as I would if I was straight. In terms of just sort of lifestyle support, you know, like young mothers with children getting together to do this. And I mean I have straight friends that have kids, but it's not the same as it would be if I had lesbian friends that had kids.

It should be noted that the children had their own support networks. Most of the children who were older than infants had friends to whom they had 'come out.' None of the friends seemed bothered by the family 'situation'; indeed, many thought it was 'neat.' Nor did the friends' parents appear concerned about the lesbian families. Whether this was an example of what Stebbins (1988: 13) calls 'habitual tolerance' (a superficial tolerance of something that does not seem threatening), or whether it was indicative of 'enlightened tolerance' (meaning that the parents had a deeper understanding and appreciation of the family form) is impossible to tell. Whatever the parents' attitudes, they did not impede friendship. The children of lesbian families did, however, carefully select their confidants. None revealed their family situation to all of their classmates, for example. Nonetheless, each was able to maintain what appeared to be a 'normal' friendship network.

DOMESTIC ROLES

Contrary to the stereotype that lesbian couples sort themselves into traditionally feminine and masculine roles and behaviours, *every* woman in my sample said that domestic tasks were shared equally in terms of quantity and divided in terms of each partner's areas of ability and enjoyment. Most couples shared fairly evenly tasks such as housecleaning and cooking. In homes with older children, the children were expected to help with housework, do their own laundry, and sometimes cook one supper a week.

In the D.I. families, whoever was home and available would usually perform the bulk of the housecleaning. Because the partners tended to take turns staying at home, there was no permanent division of labour. The following responses were typical of the D.I. mothers:

We lead really hectic lives. We both have shift jobs, and so we get weeks of total shutdown where neither of us [is] doing anything. And then we get weeks where one of us is working but the house is a pigsty, so someone's got to do it, right. We don't really split the roles. It's just whatever gets done, whoever does it does it.

With Steven [baby] now it's whoever is home does most of the housekeeping and cooking and things like that. And so, you know, I mean Iris is a far better cook than me, but I'm cooking so it's a bit of a struggle, but it's okay. And we're really really conscious of gender stereotypical roles.

None of the blended families had pre-school-age children, so no partner stayed home for this reason. All the women were employed or in school. Two of the couples had occasional housekeepers to 'keep things under control,' while the rest divided housework between them (again, according to 'abilities and availabilities').

Each woman said that she and her partner performed the tasks they most preferred and then divided equally the less pleasant ones. I asked the respondents to specify what tasks were divided according to enjoyment. It became clear that not one of these women was stereotypically 'feminine' or 'masculine' in terms of their interests or abilities. The woman who enjoyed cooking and sewing might also be the one who kept the family cars running and built the shed in the backyard.

By sharing equally in the domestic labour, these women managed to overcome the gender-typed role-playing in which they had seen their parents participate. Iris said that she and Blaire made a conscious effort not to get trapped in rigid roles:

[We are] really sensitive to roles in the house because, as far as domestic roles go, I'm more handy than Blaire is and she's more particular about cleanliness than I am, and so it's really easy for us to fall into those roles. But we've challenged each other to accept those roles for ourselves. Like if Blaire was hanging a mirror or something, there was a time I would have just stepped in and said, 'Here, let me do that.' But now we're at the point where we expect each other to do it for ourselves. Because I would always step in and Blaire would never be able to hang a picture or whatever. And the same goes for things around the house, you know, if Blaire let me get away with it, she'd do the laundry all the time. So we really force each other to do what has to be done and not depend so much on roles.

These women's lives point out the erroneousness of notions about the biological bases of domestic and social roles. They also belie the stereotype that lesbian couples emulate heterosexual roles by playing 'butch' and 'femme' roles (although individuals or couples may *choose* to do so). Just as there is no necessary link between biology and sexual orientation, there is no necessary link between biology or sexual orientation and domestic or parenting roles.

The key roles in these lesbian families are the parenting roles. As revealed in chapters 4 and 5, parenting roles were not divided the same in D.I. and blended families. The D.I. mothers tried to divide mothering evenly, with each partner performing the same tasks with identical frequency. Many said that the only difference in the mothering roles they played was that some of the biological mothers breastfed, which, of course, the non-biological mothers could not do. In the blended families, the biological mothers often performed the bulk of the mothering tasks for their children, leaving the stepmothers to try to establish themselves in the home in general and in some type of parenting role in particular.

Once a couple decided if and how they would co-parent within the home, they had to decide if and how they would present themselves as co-parents outside the home. Having children brings people into greater contact with such public institutions as schools, day-care centres, clinics, and hospitals. Each couple had to decide whether to be 'out' in these places. All the D.I. couples felt strongly that they should clearly present themselves as co-parents. On school records and hospital documentation, for example, they scratched out 'name of father' and wrote in 'co-parent.' Four of the six D.I. couples had infants, and so their contact with some of these institutions was limited. The other two couples, however, had presented themselves as co-parents throughout their children's lives. One of these couples had two grown children, the other a four year old. Not only did both couples present themselves as co-parents on paper, but they were also equally and openly involved as parents in their children's public lives. Almost never had they encountered openly discriminatory attitudes or behaviour on the part of teachers or parents of their children's friends.

Each of the D.I. couples had decided that it would be wrong to tell the child that they were his or her parents inside the home and then present themselves in some other relationship outside the home. Tina's description of how she and Rose approached this issue was typical of all the D.I. mothers:

We had decided from the beginning that when Tim was born we would be up-front and open about it [their relationship to each other and to him]. His day care knows. When he goes to elementary school, they'll know because we feel that, I mean it will be [at] his discretion whether to disclose or not to his peers. But we are not going to make our lifestyle something that he should see as something to be ashamed of. We'll be positive about it, and hopefully he'll gain security from that [and be able] to deal with it in whatever manner he wants. We would hope that he would feel comfortable about it – you know, not to have to hide it – but we wouldn't condemn him if he felt the need to do that.

Although each of the D.I. couples had decided that it was important that significant parties be made aware of their relationship and of the fact that they were co-mothering, it was sometimes difficult to determine *which* parties were significant. They had to decide who was worth telling and who was not. Denise described such a situation:

Once we started getting babysitters in – fourteen-year-old girls – I kept thinking, 'Oh my God,' you know. One of the girls, she brought her mother over, and they came in the house and I could just see the mother going, 'Is this girl a sister? How does she fit into the picture?' You know, you can just see the questions going through their mind, and you think, 'Well now, should we just plain go ahead and say, you know, we're gay?' But then it's like people don't walk around going 'Well, you know, we're heterosexual' ... You just don't know quite how to deal with non-permanent relationships – that's the place that it gets a little tough. So you come up with the answers as you need to.

For Noreen, one of the problems with being out as lesbian parents is that people tend to think of lesbian families as different or not quite 'real':

People perceive them [lesbian families] to be different, but they're not. You know, it's just two people parenting that are loving their kids. And that's it, you know, and there shouldn't be any discussion beyond that except acceptance. You know, like if you just accept the family then that's all you need.

Fear of rejection was one of the factors that kept many of the blended family couples from presenting themselves publicly as co-parents. Another crucial factor was that these couples very often were *not* co-parents in the sense of sharing parenting tasks and authority. Almost all the biological mothers in these families had decided against listing their partners as 'co-parent' on school documents and the like. While the stepmothers were sometimes invited to school plays and baseball games, they were rarely invited to parent–teacher interviews. This was often an area of contention between the women, resulting in the stepmothers' feeling even more excluded from the lives of the children they often cared deeply about and had some considerable hand in raising.

RAISING BOYS[1]

The common belief among the D.I. mothers that they had an 85 per cent

1 The absence of a section on raising girls should not be taken to suggest that either I or my respondents find nothing interesting, special, unique, or challenging about raising girls. Quite the contrary. However, girls did not occupy the potentially controversial position within the lesbian and feminist communities that boys sometimes did. Mothers of daughters also did not encounter the widespread concern about having a male role model in the house that mothers of sons often did. And mothers of daughters were less concerned than mothers of sons about their ability to raise a feminist child. Perhaps it was easier for mothers of daughters to envision the sort of feminist woman they wanted their daughters to become than for mothers of sons to envision a realistic feminist man and then figure out how to go about raising a son accordingly. We must, of course, bear in mind that not all lesbian women are feminist, and so not all lesbian mothers have to struggle with this question.

A myth that many lesbian mothers of daughters must face, whether or not they are chance of having boys using donor insemination was supported by family composition (although, of course, we must bear in mind that this a small sample, not necessarily representative of trends in the broader population). Of the eight children in this group, five were conceived by self-insemination and three through heterosexual intercourse. Of the five S.I. babies, one is a girl. This ratio might be explained by the method of fertility charting and the nature of sperm. Unless a woman has an extremely regular cycle, she generally cannot know when she is two or three days before ovulation. Basal temperature measurements and commercially packaged ovulation predictor kits can tell a woman only when she is ovulating or has ovulated. At best, she can determine the time twelve to twenty-four hours before her 'peak time.' Male-producing sperm swim faster and die sooner than female-producing sperm. Therefore, if a woman were to inseminate at peak time, the male-producing sperm would have a better chance of reaching the ovum, whereas if a woman were to inseminate two to three days before ovulation, most of the sperm still alive would be female-producing. Thus, because D.I. women are inseminating so close to ovulation, they have a much higher chance (although not necessarily an 85 per cent chance) of giving birth to boys (Pies 1988: 180).

Although I do not want to create the impression that lesbians are anti-male, some women did believe it would be easier to raise a feminist girl than a feminist boy. Some respondents had also encountered members of the lesbian and feminist communities who are separatist. These women want nothing to do with men, and believe that lesbian mothers of boys are 'raising the oppressor.' None of the women in my sample associated with separatist women, although they had occasionally heard separatist sentiments voiced.

It is not uncommon for both lesbian and heterosexual feminists, on

---

feminist, is that lesbian mothers will raise lesbian daughters. None of the women in my sample had explicit expectations concerning their children's sexual orientation, and none were working to influence their children's sexual identity one way or the other. There is no evidence that the proportions of homosexuality and heterosexuality in children of lesbian women and gay men are any different than those in the children of heterosexuals. It makes sense that simply being raised in a lesbian or gay home would not have a determining influence on the development of a child's sexual identity. After all, most lesbians and gay men were raised in heterosexual homes and, furthermore, were heavily steeped in heterosexual culture during their formative years (and beyond). The development of sexual identity is clearly not simply a matter of suggestion or role modelling.

occasion, to seek out women-only spaces and events. Such major events as the take-back-the-night marches and the Michigan Women's Folk Festival[2] have been known to bar the entrance of males older than a set age (which could be as young as three). Although women might be able to find a babysitter for a night while they go to a march, it is unlikely they would be willing to leave their sons for a week or more while they attended the Michigan festival. Many mothers, both lesbian and heterosexual, are thus excluded from such events. Whereas the interest in women-only spaces is understandable, it is possible that the barring of males serves to perpetuate and reinforce the stereotypical view that once a boy reaches a certain age, an *inherent* (dangerous) masculinity sets in and he is no longer just a child – he is a man. This view can be especially troubling to those women who are trying to raise 'non-traditional' boys.

None of the D.I. mothers was upset over the prospect of raising a boy, although it did present a couple of particular challenges. One concerned the issue of male role models. All the mothers heard from family members, friends, acquaintances, and strangers that, in order to develop 'normally,' a boy needs a male role model. Each of the couples struggled with this question. Several reached the conclusion that it was unnecessary to have a male in the house because society itself is so male dominated. Additionally, these boys would come into contact with a range of males throughout their lives. As Rose observed:

Our society has enough male role models out there. There are male teachers. There are male swim instructors. There are all these males in helping professions now, in teaching professions, that there weren't when I was in school. It was really rare to get a kindergarten teacher who was male, and now you see that quite often. Um, plus Tina's got a brother who loves to spend time with Tim, so with our families and with society I'm not worried.

Many of the women were unwilling to seek out a male to spend time with their sons just for the sake of having a male role model. Getting an 'uncle at large,' for example, seemed unnecessary, and some women said that they would not involve their sons with organizations such as Big Brothers and Uncles at Large, which openly discriminate against homosexual people by refusing them as volunteers. None of the women

2 This annual event attracts thousands of women from across North America and other parts of the world. For some women, the trip to Michigan is a sort of pilgrimage.

were very concerned that their sons would suffer from not having a male in the home, but some were getting tired of receiving lectures on the subject. It appears that part of the discomfort that conventional society has with lesbian families stems not from the mothers' lesbianism, but from the fact that there is no male presence or influence in the home. As Tina noted, 'Women have always needed a man to validate their existence, and the family especially is the cornerstone of male domination.' Is it also possible, in our mother-blaming culture, that the presence of two mothers is unthinkable given the received wisdom that one mother is all you need to bungle your life?

The other challenge facing lesbian women who are raising boys is that, if the women are feminist (which everyone in my sample said she was), they see it as their duty to raise a non-traditional male. Tina explained:

There probably is a driving desire within lesbian parents of males to want to have a feminist son. So no war toys and this and that and trying to instil all of these wonderful virtues in a male. And I don't know how successful that can be. But I think that probably, because you don't want to be seen raising your own oppression, that comes into it. So I think there is a part of you that [says] 'My son is not going to do this. He's going to be a sensitive, caring, responsible human being. He will not oppress anyone.'

Iris believed that it was to her son's benefit to be raised by two lesbian mothers:

I think that we have more things to look forward to because we are relatively enlightened about a lot of different aspects of life – like discrimination, racism, sexism, and things like that – that a lot of heterosexual couples aren't exactly enlightened about. And I think we have an opportunity to pass that on to him and make him a better person, you know a child that we could consider a better person. And I think that's a benefit from our lives.

However committed the mothers were to raising a non-traditional male, the tasks could be a formidable one, and there were no guarantees of success. Janine, a biological mother in a blended family, described her experiences raising her son to adulthood:

I raised my son differently, not because I was lesbian but because I was feminist. Because I believed in equality and I believed in equal respect for both sexes. Um,

I raised mine differently because of who I was. I believed in equality for people, I despised racial intolerance. And I would expect of him that he would be as tolerant of gays and lesbians as he is of blacks and Chinese, and accept people as they are people and not because they happen to have a label attached to them. And I'd say I raised him, ah well, I tried to raise him as more of a pacifist. But because he lives in the male society, and has to be the macho guy that he's supposed to be, he still goes out and will go to a bar, and if he drinks too much will end up getting into a physical fight, which I wouldn't want him to do, you know. I tried not to buy him a lot of guns, but he would make them out of his lego. You know, I tried to teach him to turn the other cheek, and to be intolerant of discrimination, and be more willing to solve conflicts with words as opposed to fists – but it didn't necessarily work.

It seems likely that the sons of my respondents will grow up to be as varied and as 'good' or 'bad' as anyone else's children, although they will perhaps be more familiar with feminist ideals than many other boys. What we do know is that if increasing numbers of lesbian women have children through donor insemination, and if the majority of them have sons, a significant proportion of the lesbian population will be raising boys. Thus, in twenty to thirty years, a significant cross-section of the population of young men in North America will have been raised by lesbian mothers. The social impact of this demographic change will be interesting to observe.

CHALLENGES AND BENEFITS: BLENDED FAMILIES

Because of the social stigma attached to lesbianism, many blended family couples kept their family lives closeted – usually, as we have seen, out of concern for the children. Although one family, including the children, was completely 'out' (and had never suffered negative repercussions because of it), none of the other women were willing to assume the risks associated with coming out.

Related to concerns about being out was the realization by previously childless women that having children put them in much greater contact with the public world. Dealing with children's schools, friends, and leisure activities put the relationship under much greater public scrutiny than generally happens for childless couples. This made staying in the closet for the sake of the children all the more difficult – but also, many women believed, all the more necessary.

The public gaze was not the only gaze to which the couples were subject. Whereas biological mothers were used to sharing their lives with their children, previously childless women were surprised by the extent to which the relationship had to accommodate itself to the presence of children. 'It's sometimes really frustrating,' Laura said, 'but you can only do your arguing or your intimate kinds of discussing or have sex together at certain times in certain contexts.'

Lack of acknowledgment in the heterosexual world was often exacerbated by relatives who could not accept a family member's lesbianism. What emerges is a picture of families living in varying degrees of isolation and 'closetedness,' and sometimes receiving minimal social support. As Carol explained:

We're [not] necessarily acknowledged as a family needing support and that sort of thing. I think probably quite the contrary ... If Laura and I were mixed-gender parents I think it would be different.

One might assume that if recognition and support were not forthcoming from the heterosexual world, then these families would rely more heavily upon their lesbian friends for support. Although most tried to find support within the lesbian community, a few encountered total incomprehension on the part of their lesbian friends as to why they (especially the previously childless women) would become part of a blended family. Although lesbian friends might have been willing to acknowledge that a family had been formed, and that there were difficulties maintaining it, they were sometimes hesitant to offer real assistance. Carol elaborated:

One thing too that we've noticed is people are quite willing to acknowledge how hard it is, you know, because we don't have enough money really to support our household, and that sort of thing. But nobody's really willing to get involved in that. You know, like, they're, they're very much *our* children ... Although they acknowledged how hard it must be for us, it was *our* problem. It was very much ours.

Nonetheless, as we have seen, many couples reported that their friends, lesbian and heterosexual, were the closest they came to having an extended family.

Some stepmothers were uncomfortable with the primacy of the children in the lives of the biological mothers. Often the biological mother had to struggle to balance the needs of the lesbian relationship with the needs of the relationship with the children. Laura, a biological mother, stated that one of the biggest challenges she and Carol faced was

spontaneity and setting priorities and remembering to leave enough time for the relationship ... I think when Carol and I first got involved ... my relationship with the kids and the kids' needs had to come first, at the expense of everything else. And really, I've had to learn to honour the relationship too, [and to realize] that it is important and it isn't going to just be there because I wish it would be. It needs time and it's just as important. That's probably been the biggest thing, juggling all of that. It got a lot easier once I figured out you have to kind of just do it.

Although the need to juggle priorities can exist in any blended-family situation, the women in my sample attributed certain compromises that they had to make to the fact that they were two women – and often two *mothers* – trying to co-exist. These women were faced with the difficult task of trying to reconcile two different approaches to mothering. In some cases, the result was a lack of co-parenting, which some women felt was to their children's detriment. Daphne said:

[Nanette and I] see our kids, both sets of kids, as losers in this relationship. That the kids aren't gaining anything from the relationship. Financially, her kids have gained. But that's the only way in which they have gained really ... because I don't have a relationship with [Nanette's children]. So they have this person in the house, um, who they're not really relating to. Basically, there's very little communication between the children and I.

Some of the challenges faced by these families were related to the women's lesbianism, and some were not.

Christine offered a general overview of the drawbacks to lesbian family life:

I think the primary thing is that children eat up a great deal of your life and your soul, and there isn't as much left over as we perhaps would like. We said we dream about the day they're finally gone. There's always inherent issues of disclosure, protecting the kids from disclosure. The secretness. Lack of community acknowledgment as parents.

Carol articulated more particular problems as she described the challenges she faced in trying to create a family with Laura and Laura's children:

Your time is not your own. Um, things like, you know, just hanging out, being able to talk with Laura about whatever we're interested in, is around someone else's schedule. Never mind things like sex, you know. Constantly having to do errands and pick people up and that sort of thing drives me wild. They [kids] don't pick up after themselves, you know. When you look in the fridge to have something you knew was there, it's never there. It's always eaten. They're grubby creatures, you know – their rooms are scary. We make a point of their rooms being theirs until the smell starts wafting out into the main part of the house. They never do their chores. Well, they eventually do their chores, but you have to talk to them about it for fourteen hundred hours. They play rotten music. My relationship with Laura ... I'm in a relationship with someone who clearly has two other relationships. Whereas my relationship with the kids is *aside from*, you know. It's not a primary relationship in the same way that my relationship with Laura is. But her relationship with the kids is primary as well as her relationship with me. So I have to share.

Despite the many challenges and issues they faced, the women derived from their membership in a blended family benefits that they did not feel would otherwise have come their way. Many women said that life in a blended family contributed to their personal growth and development. Several women who had been previously childless found that parenting, whatever form it assumed, required them to be less self-involved. Daphne said:

[I'm] glad I didn't have any kids 'cause I really learned a lot by not having kids. I didn't give up myself to meet a bunch of other people's needs, and I feel good about that. And I know now that living with [Sharon's kids] that I'm perfectly capable of giving up and compromising, and I feel really good about that too.

Carol described how the presence of children had affected her own development:

It has helped me not take myself so seriously, not take my relationship so seriously. It's helped me to not be so selfish, I think. I think it's really good, but part of me kind of goes, 'Why would you think that?' you know. But yeah, I think it has been *exceptionally* good for me to have these kids in my life.

Many women felt that having children diluted the emotional intensity of the lesbian relationship, or, at the very least, made it impossible for the partners to be involved only with each other. The presence of chil-

dren forced an emotional balance they had seldom experienced in earlier lesbian relationships where there had been a real possibility of
'mergence.' As Barbara put it:

Maybe it [being in a childed family] normalizes the relationship. It doesn't
become this awe-inspiring unique little thing that the two of you have, right, it's
just a part of relating. You're part of a family instead, or part of the world,
instead of two people off in isolation.

For some women – especially the biological mothers – it was not the
contact with children that was especially new and important to them; it
was claiming a lesbian identity and sharing their parenting within a
lesbian relationship. 'I'm more me now,' Nanette said. 'I can be who I
wish to be now that I'm in this relationship.' Several women expressed
their relief that they did not have to deal with men as partners or co-
parents:

I can see that if it came to my kids and I lived with a man, that he would expect
to have the bottom line.

I don't have to put up with the layers and layers of male bullshit. You know,
you think you're getting one thing and you're getting something else ... and
the manipulation. And the language problems. You know, women and men
don't speak the same language. It's English but I don't know what they do to
it ... And the power: the push–pull is not there; [the need] to control is just not
there.

A man would more likely have the tendency to come in and become the authority. He would expect to be the authority in the relationship. Um, not all men, but
likely most men would expect to operate that way.

One of the most appealing features of lesbian co-parenting, for many
women, was that it allowed them unprecedented equality in a relationship with another adult. As Janine explained:

I think it's great because ... the traditional roles don't get in the way. You can
divide the responsibilities and areas of responsibility by abilities, and availabilities, whereas that wasn't necessarily so in a heterosexual relationship, and particularly when I was married. You know, we were still in fairly strong
traditional roles where it was expected the man would go out to work and it

was expected you would stay home. And it was expected that he would fix this and it was expected that you would take care of the house. In special circumstances, if there was company coming, he would do some of the housework to help clean up because there was somebody coming over. But on a regular basis, that was my job. And that sort of thing. So I think it's much more equal.

Many of the previously childless women found that being part of a family brought stability to their lives. Marda said:

It [involvement with a woman who had a child] was kind of like a bonus, or a kind of adding a bit of stability to my life that I had not had for a long time, or really in actuality before.

Similarly, Barbara revealed:

I get stability because, um, I'm a real workaholic and I was not, um, it's really nice to have people to come home and share things with. That's what I get out of it. Frustration too, but I get satisfaction, you know, sharing things with other people. I have a family now, and it's something that's very important to have ... It's stable and it's allowing me to be happy, be more aware of myself, to discover myself more as a person.

Andrea was among those women who genuinely enjoyed being with children and being able to play a role in their lives:

I get a lot of enjoyment out of watching people grow, whether they're adults or whether they're kids. You know, just hearing about how far Charlene [stepdaughter] is coming in school ... I mean it's just really neat to me to watch that ... being able to appreciate the gifts in her ... I don't know where it comes from, but I feel proud to be walking around the grocery store [with Charlene] or wherever we happen to be. It's just kind of a neat feeling for me ... I don't know if it's because I think other people think that she's my daughter and that's something that I want, and so that's a way that I can do it.

The benefits of life in a blended lesbian family were experienced by the children as well. Some women believed that the new family status energized a family situation that had grown somewhat stagnant. Others felt that a female co-parent was better for the children than a male co-parent would have been. Sharon stated:

It's better that it's a woman because my kids were used to having, their parent *was* a woman. Now they have two, so it's twice as good. It probably made it easier.

The vast majority of respondents believed that it was a very positive thing for children to grow up in such 'alternative' families. The view that life in a blended lesbian family would expose the children to options, and thereby open their minds, was expressed by several women:

Inadvertently, children – both male and female – begin to see a more androgynous gender as opposed to it always being dad things and mom things. But moms can do things that they thought only dads did and vice versa.

Because they can accept us, then they can accept all kinds of differences in other kids, in other people. So I think growing up in a 'non-normal' family will teach the kids more acceptance.

I think that homosexuals, whether they're lesbians or gay men, because they've had to go through a process and have had to challenge society, to say 'I'm different,' and if they have come to the acceptance of their sexuality, they're more, um, they're better adjusted people than the average Joe on the street. And they're less limited because they've gone through – I mean that's a major struggle, right. So because of that they can transfer that to their kids, so their kids will be better adjusted and will have less limitations, limiting beliefs, or whatever.

CHALLENGES AND BENEFITS: D.I. FAMILIES

As one might expect with new parents, D.I. mothers were often surprised by the considerable labour involved in meeting a baby's needs. Their social lives were profoundly changed as they gave up many old social activities and sought out new ones in which babies could be included. The baby became the centre of the couple's attention, and they sometimes had to remind themselves to spend some time and energy on each other and on themselves. These challenges are not unique to lesbian parents. Almost all the difficulties that are unique to lesbian families can be traced to the social perceptions of this family form.

Nearly every woman said that once she had a baby, 'spontaneity' became impossible. Every aspect of her life had to be planned around the baby. Again, this is not unusual for any young couple with a baby. But the frustrations that the women in my sample sometimes felt with respect to parental responsibilities were exacerbated by the frequent lack of understanding within their lesbian social milieu. Lesbian couples having babies is a relatively new practice in the lesbian community, and that community very often simply fails to understand all that having a baby entails. Many women said that friends would continue to phone them with such questions as 'Do you want to go to the dance tonight?' They did not seem to comprehend that parents of young children cannot 'pick up and go out' at a moment's notice. Several women said that, instead of trying to plan events in advance, some friends simply stopped calling. Nancy described how difficult it was for her and Elly to be parents while simultaneously maintaining an active role within the lesbian community:

I think that we, in some ways we could become isolated from our lesbian community because we can't do the things in some ways. Like we don't have the spontaneity to go out to supper if everybody decides to go, or play football on Sunday afternoons. We have to organize who's going to take care of Astrid. We can't both play unless we get a sitter. There's things that we just can't do anymore and that lesbians don't have to even think about, like it's not in their reality at all. There's been situations where I've wanted to just have the ability to be camping with a whole group of lesbians and walk down the beach, when there they go and I've got to figure out who's looking after Astrid, you know. We have to discuss who's got her this time and what's going on. Is it nap time or is she hungry or what? And just trying to get that understanding across to lesbians, like what it's like to have a kid. One time when we were out at the lake recently and I spent forty-five minutes trying to get Astrid to go to sleep 'cause it was a different place and she was completely crabbed out and ready for a sleep. But she wouldn't go to sleep, so I walked around outside for forty-five minutes and brought her in, and there was five women sitting in the room and they just couldn't contain themselves. They started laughing and goofing off and Astrid woke up, of course, and I was so angry, I was so pissed off. And it was like you guys just can't understand what that's about, you know, what it's like to work at that for an hour and then have it sabotaged, and how tied in I am because if she sleeps I get some time. And so that was a learning process for a lot of the women there, 'cause I got really mad. And then I felt guilty for getting mad, and then I felt guilty for being there, like why was I even there, 'cause, you know, here I am imposing this on them.

Fortunately, close lesbian friends were often amenable to being educated about the demands of parenthood, and thereby became important support figures for the family.

The greatest challenges faced by D.I. families came from outside the lesbian community. Living in a world where the common assumption is that everyone is heterosexual sometimes places these families in awkward situations. As Iris explained:

I always feel like when we're [Iris and Blaire] out walking together, unless we're holding hands, I always feel like people look at us like we're sisters or something, and I just kind of laugh at it myself, although I do think about it when I do get that look of recognition in people's eyes. It's obvious that not many people assume we're lesbians, because we have a baby ... I think we'd be flattered if somebody assumed that we were lesbians, you know. It would be like 'Wow, society has taken a leap forward.'

The assumption of universal heterosexuality puts lesbian mothers in the position of having to repeatedly 'come out' if they want their family arrangement to be at all comprehensible to outsiders. We have already seen that many of these couples present themselves as 'mother' and 'co-parent' on all documentation regarding the child, and that one of the greatest difficulties they face is determining who is worth coming out to and who is not. Coming out is never easy, even without children, because people's responses cannot usually be anticipated. Each of the women believed, however, that it was important that the children not feel that there was anything wrong with their families. Thus it became a challenge for the women to become comfortable about coming out. Iris said:

My big thing now is saying to people that I was artificially inseminated. And really, you know, what it is for me right now is having to say that and telling myself that I myself can cope with that, admitting to people that Steven doesn't have a father, but that I was artificially inseminated. And I feel it's really important for me to be able to say that if I want him to be able to cope with it when he's older.

Elly expressed similar feelings about the issue of coming out:

One of my biggest concerns is that Astrid not be shamed or not feel shame about her family, and so that requires us to be brave and strong, and sometimes I'm not brave and strong. My sort of ultimate worry is that one day someone will say to Astrid, 'Is Nancy your mother?' and she'll say no, or Nancy will say no, or I'll say, 'no, I am,' because we're in a threatening situation or it's not safe. What will that do to Astrid? 'Well, this was my mother. I thought she was my mother.

Now you tell me she's not my mother' ... I think we've made the commitment that when Astrid is involved and aware of what's going on that we be clear that we are co-parenting her, that I'm her biological mother, Nancy is her other mother or her co-parent. And we've made a commitment to co-parent. Doing that, not necessarily expecting that that reveals the sexual relationship or just our relationship, but that reveals our relationship to Astrid and that's what's important to Astrid and whoever is asking.

Related to concerns about coming out was the need to prepare the child for discrimination that he or she might face as a result of the family's composition. All the women believed in the importance of taking measures to ensure that the children felt secure in their families and confident in themselves. Many women said there was a fine line between sensitizing a child to possible problems and scaring him or her. 'I think that all we can really do is tell him [son] what to expect,' Iris said, 'and tell him our experiences, and be honest and let him know that he can talk to us about anything that happens.' Blaire added, 'The big thing is, we don't want to instil a sense of fear in him [such] that people are going to hate him.'

Because lesbianism is stigmatized in Canadian society, all the women found themselves, at one time or another, having to defend their right to have children and their ability to raise them. Evelyn said that she and Kim got tired of

having our right to be parents constantly questioned. Constantly, like no matter who you mention it to – 'oh, Kim is going to have a baby' – [they say], 'Well, do you think that's right?' So you've got to [go through] your whole political spiel with anybody you give this information to as if they have a right to decide whether you should be a parent or not.

The D.I. mothers said that not only did they have to defend the 'normalcy' of their families to friends, relatives, and complete strangers, but they also had to challenge institutions that conceived of 'family' only in terms of the traditional heterosexual nuclear family. Many places and events that offer 'family' admission rates do not regard lesbian families as families. As a result of the efforts of some of the women in my sample, a few establishments in Calgary, such as leisure centres and swimming pools, have modified their definition of family from 'a man and woman and their children' to 'two adults and children.' Many places, however, have yet to make this change.

What this means for lesbian families is that to live a 'normal' family life, they must constantly tell people that they *are* a normal family. Educating others proved to be a fatiguing process for some of the women, including Tina:

I think the hardest part is always educating [people], you know. And sometimes you get tired of saying, 'This is my family, and this is why we are the way we are, and this is what we do,' you know. And sometimes you sit back and go, 'Well, I don't get why you don't get it.' And we just keep slogging away, and it's for Tim's benefit mainly, but I mean it's for the benefit of anyone really that comes in contact with our family. But you do, you get tired educating people all the time.

Other women, however, enjoyed playing the role of educator and shaking up people's preconceptions.

Lack of social recognition of lesbian families means that there is no recognition of the role played by the non-biological mother. As we have seen, D.I. couples often have to inform their friends and relatives that they are *both* mothers to the child. The absence of social recognition presents an ongoing battle for these families.

Like the blended-family mothers, however, the D.I. mothers also believed that the benefits of this family form outweighed the challenges. Several said that the presence of two mothers meant that parenting could be divided more equally than they had seen it divided in many heterosexual households. Moreover, the sharing of mothering duties gave each woman an understanding of motherhood that she would not have received under a less equitable division of labour. Iris explained:

Blaire's home with him [baby] in the summer, and then in the fall I'll be home with him all winter. And it's been beneficial for us because now we both know what it's like to stay home with a baby, and there's no way we can take each other for granted now. I think, you know, in heterosexual couples when the husband comes home and goes, 'Oh, the dishes aren't done. What have you been doing, watching soap operas?' You know, there's no way that we could say that because we know.

Several women were convinced that having two mothers made for greater consistency in the parenting the child received. Again, Iris explained:

I think it's really hard not to generalize because I see us as having female qualities, and when you consider traditional female qualities – nurturing and gentle-
ness and caring – then I include that as an asset. You know, as opposed to
raising a child with a man. You know, I think that there's some consistency
because we both have those qualities. And I'm not saying that men don't have
those qualities, but I don't know many who do. And I think there's more consistency in the way we raise him, between the two of us, because we both have
those qualities.

Most of the respondents also believed that they were able to have an
equitable division of labour because they were two women sharing the
tasks.

Some couples observed that one advantage the D.I. family had over
the blended family was that the former did not have to deal with the
step-parenting issues; both women had been mothers to the children
since birth. As Noreen explained:

That's one of the good things [about] having children within your relationship.
The kids have never yelled, 'Well, you're not my mother' or 'Who are you' or
anything like that, which would be very hurtful to her [Melanie] I think. She's
mature and I mean she could take it, but still for a non-biological parent sometimes it can be very hurtful when kids do that sort of thing. But we haven't
[encountered it], and in discipline, that kind of thing, they listen to her the same
as they do me.

For all the women, the greatest benefit of being in a D.I. family was
simply the pleasure they got from raising a child from birth, and raising
it together. Rose echoed the sentiments of all the women when she said
that the greatest reward was 'probably the self-satisfaction of nurturing
this little tiny infant and watching him grow, and knowing that at least
part of his knowledge you're helping to shape.'

For women like Blaire, the challenges that accompanied lesbian D.I.
parenting were inextricably linked to its rewards:

The benefits are the challenge of everything, you know. I mean if I was with a
man I wouldn't explore it as I am with a woman. The sense of freedom that we
can sort of be anything we want to Steven. It's more sort of if I could say proac-
tive. Or it's thinking instead of reacting. I mean, you know, we think maybe
more than we really need to, but we think about everything and we don't, we

think about how things will affect Steven probably more than heterosexual people. But I think sometimes more than sexual orientation our actual personalities, who we are, has a lot more to do with parenting than being a lesbian.

FIGHTING FOR THE FAMILY

Being raised by two mothers is not identical to being raised by one mother, by a mother and a father, by one father, or by two fathers. Sharing mothering with another woman is not identical to mothering alone or mothering with a male partner. There are three dimensions along which these differences are meaningful for lesbian families in Canada:

1 both parents are women;
2 the parents are homosexual;
3 the family exists in a heterosexist, patriarchal, homophobic society.

The first two dimensions were not seen by my respondents to be problematic in and of themselves. Nor were they perceived to negatively affect the quality or type of life and upbringing the children experienced. Two women negotiating shared parenting roles may face different challenges and enjoy different rewards than might a man and a woman engaged in such negotiation, but this does not render lesbian families fundamentally different from, or alien to, other types of family. Often what distinguishes lesbian families, and life within them, from other types of families are the repercussions of the attitudinal and legal context within which they exist.

We have seen that lesbians, as lesbians, can be marginalized by their families of origin, by the society at large, and by other mothers. They are marginalized by their invisibility, which derives from the assumption of universal heterosexuality. As mothers they can be marginalized within the lesbian community due to a lack of recognition, respect, or understanding of their parenting choices. Lesbian families are marginalized by mainstream beliefs that families are, and should always be, created by heterosexuals; that parenting roles consist of 'mother' and 'father' or something closely analogous (such as stepmother and stepfather); that there is a correct way and time to become a mother (e.g., within a heterosexual marriage); and that only certain women deserve to become mothers (generally, heterosexual married women).

Lesbian women, and lesbian family members, encounter on a daily basis the manifestations of heterosexist thinking, ranging from the attitudes of friends, family, acquaintances, co-workers and strangers, through media portrayals of lesbian women and gay men, to discriminatory treatment within major social institutions such as education, medicine, and law. North America has seen dramatic increases in gay and lesbian rights activism over the last thirty years, especially since the Stonewall rebellion of 1969. It is striking that much of the opposition to gay and lesbian legal equality comes from those who claim that gays and lesbians are a threat to 'the family.' This perspective not only renders invisible healthy and functioning lesbian families, but it also implies that such a thing cannot and should not exist.

Such is the ideological milieu within which lesbian families exist in Canada. The legal system, informed by the dominant heterosexist ideology, serves to define and bolster 'the family' while often penalizing lesbian families and leaving them vulnerable to attack. Lesbians cannot be legally married in Canada, which means that partners are denied spousal benefits, pay more tax, and are left in a precarious legal situation regarding inheritances. The lack of legal recognition of the non-biological mother leaves her emotionally, legally, and financially vulnerable; in fact, it renders her completely powerless as a parent outside of the home.

It is little wonder, then, that lesbian women have banded together to fight not only for their own recognition and equal treatment under the law but also for the recognition and protection of their families. In 1985, the equality provision of the Canadian Charter of Rights and Freedoms (section 15) came into effect. Although 'sexual orientation' is not specified as a protected ground, it has been accepted as a ground analogous to those that *are* listed in the section. Canadian gays and lesbians have used section 15 to challenge discriminatory legislation. Herman (1994) points out that '[m]uch, although not all, of the resulting litigation turned on definitions of 'family' or 'spouse' within various federal and provincial statutes' (27).

There is little consistency among the provinces in their responses to these challenges. For example, in May 1995 the Supreme Court of Canada reaffiremed that sexual orientation was a protected ground under the Charter, but ruled that the denial of spousal pension benefits to a B.C. couple did not constitute discrimination because the couple were not married. Two weeks earlier, the Ontario Supreme Court had ruled that lesbians and gays could not be discriminated against in terms of adopting children.

Most major cities and many smaller communities in Canada have at least one lesbian and gay rights group. These groups fight for numerous changes, including coverage in human rights legislation, fair representation in the media, protection from discrimination and hate crimes, health-care coverage for partners, spousal benefits, and legal recognition and protection of lesbian and gay partnerships. Although these groups often are not fighting explicitly for the sake of lesbian and gay *families*, it is no coincidence that much of the opposition to them arises from 'pro-family,' anti-gay factions.

Anti-gay activists are always raising the spectres of paedophilia and the drafting of innocents into the 'homosexual lifestyle.' But these are not the threats that lesbians and gays pose to 'the family.' The threat is to heterosexual, patriarchal privilege, a large component of which is financial, and of which the traditional heterosexual, middle-class, white, nuclear family is the cornerstone. Legal marriage, legal status for parents, spousal benefits, pension benefits, spousal health-care coverage, and tax breaks for married and common-law couples are manifestations of the institutional ballast that surrounds 'the family.' These privileges not only protect families but also serve to define them.

Although legislation varies across Canada, for the most part lesbian and gay families are unrecognized and unprotected. In response to this situation, some lesbian and gay parents have gone beyond the established political-action groups to create groups that specifically address the needs of lesbian and gay families. From 1978 to 1987, for example, the Lesbian Mothers' Defence Fund operated out of Toronto, with regional branches in some provinces. This group – which was established to 'improve the position of lesbian mothers in society' (Stone 1990:199) – assisted lesbian mothers who were facing custody battles with their ex-spouses, and expanded its services to include social and educational activities. Although the group disbanded, other groups such as the Ontario-based Campaign for Equal Families and Foundation for Equal Families carry on the work of educating and litigating in the interests of gay and lesbian families.

It is beyond the scope of this discussion to explore the history of lesbian and gay political organizing in Canada. It is not even possible to give an overview of all the battles that are currently being fought. What is essential is that we understand that lesbian families exist in what is often either a hostile or complacently ignorant environment. In the face of ungrounded accusations that lesbians and gays are seeking special rights, lesbian mothers must struggle daily to protect and validate their families.

It is clear that life in a lesbian family is just as varied, challenging, comforting, amusing, frustrating, and rewarding as life in other kinds of families. More often than not, it is the stigma of lesbianism and lack of acknowledgment of lesbian families that make family life different for these women. Additionally, the fact of two women sharing parenting and domestic duties may have a greater influence on the tone of family life than the fact of their lesbianism ever could. It would appear that growing numbers of lesbian women are either using donor insemination or raising children conceived in prior heterosexual relationships. Popular, scientific, medical, and legal definitions of 'family' will have to acknowledge this reality.

7

Conclusion

A considerable amount of effort and thought goes into creating a family. This is true not only for lesbian women but for anyone, regardless of sexual orientation. But because 'family' is conventionally defined as a married heterosexual couple (generally with children), the work that goes into creating this social entity is often taken for granted. People tend to believe that families are not created – they simply *are*. A man and a woman marry, have children, and – lo and behold – they are a family. But nothing that a lesbian couple does makes them recognizable as a family according to the common definitions; whether they get married in a church or have children, or both, very few aspects of the process of forming a family can be taken for granted by these women.

The process of creating a lesbian family is similar to that followed by heterosexual couples, but no part of it is a given. In Canada, lesbian couples cannot legally marry, although there are some churches that will perform weddings, or commitment ceremonies, for lesbian and gay couples. Lesbian women in lesbian relationships will never accidentally find themselves pregnant. They have to make the choice and carefully plan every step of the procedure. Even once they have children, they are still not recognized as families by society at large and sometimes not even by the lesbian community itself. These obstacles are part of the social milieu in which a lesbian family exists; they serve to shape that family into a unique social entity, with its own characteristics and problems.

My concern has not been with the abstract couple as a family. It has been with the ways in which pursuing and achieving pregnancy and raising children can transform a couple into a certain type of family. We have seen that lesbian women have to make difficult decisions regarding pregnancy. Although informed and thoughtful decision-making is generally expected of *all* women in this era of reproductive choice; not all women are compelled to give as much thought to the process as lesbian women are.

We have also seen that lesbian women tend to prepare themselves emotionally and situationally before they attempt motherhood. Heterosexual women also take steps to prepare themselves, but whereas they are able to take certain steps for granted, lesbian women are not. The stable, committed relationship that society assumes in heterosexual marriages is something that lesbian women have to carefully analyze and construct for themselves. Since there is little general social or familial recognition of the lesbian relationship, and since there are no standards or rules (even within the lesbian community) by which various types and intensities of relationships can be identified, lesbian women have to determine for themselves what it *means* to have a stable and committed relationship.

Once they are satisfied with their relationship and emotional readiness, a lesbian couple can then consider other factors that appear to play a more primary role in heterosexual women's reproductive decision-making. Considerations such as financial security and career stability are relevant here. A factor that is probably of greater concern to lesbian than to heterosexual couples is the type of familial and societal support they can expect for their decision, their children, and their families. Lesbian couples often decide to have children knowing that their decision – unlike the same decision made by many heterosexual couples – might not be joyously received by their families. Lesbian women can come to play mothering roles by various routes. Some have children while in heterosexual relationships and later identify themselves as lesbian. Some become biological mothers while in a lesbian relationship, either through donor insemination or through heterosexual intercourse. Both types of mother are biological mothers and are thus included in common usage of the term 'mother.' The conventional meanings of 'stepmother' and 'adoptive mother' are not, however, as easily applicable to lesbian non-biological mothers.

As we have seen, in blended lesbian families the second woman is sometimes a type of stepparent, but she is rarely allowed, by either her partner or her partner's children, to be any type of 'mother.' There is no name for the role she plays. Each 'stepmother' in my sample had to struggle to find a place and a role for herself within the blended family. Part of the difficulty stems from the reluctance of biological mothers to share maternal authority (although they might be quite willing to share parental duties). Conversely, in lesbian D.I. families, each woman regards herself as a mother and, as such, as an individual with an equal claim to maternal knowledge and authority. For all the D.I. couples in my sample, this philosophy expressed itself most tangibly in the equitable division of mothering duties.

The presence of the non-biological mother or stepmother in each of these family types poses a substantial challenge to commonly held notions of what a mother is. By claiming that each woman, whether or not she gave birth to the child, is one of two equally primary parenting figures in the child's life, these women, especially the D.I. couples, are demanding that the rules that determine entrance to the culture of motherhood be changed to accommodate a new mothering reality. These women have made it clear that 'mother' is not merely a role or a label. It is a state of being, a perspective, an emotional connection, and a set of activities. It is a status whose achievement depends on validation by others that one *is* a mother.

That there is no acknowledged role or identity for the second (non-biological) mother in a lesbian family is one of the problems that all these women face as they try to win recognition for their family form. Certainly, there are other family forms that do not fit the conventional notion of family. Single-parent families are the fastest-growing alternative family form in North America today. According to the women in my sample, the society at large tends to perceive as single those women who are not attached to a man. It is not surprising, then, that the biological mothers were often regarded as single mothers. Indeed, census figures for single-parent families would include lesbian families since, by census classification, if a woman is not legally married to a man, she is single.

The conceptual challenge posed by lesbian families has several aspects. First, the accepted male–female pattern of parenting does not apply. The children in D.I. families also two parents, but they are both female. The children in the blended families also have two parents (who may or may not both 'mother'), and possibly three if the father is involved. The biological mother in these families is not a single mother, and the second woman is not equivalent to a father or a stepfather. Clearly, 'family' is not a self-evident concept. Although there are conventional and scientific differentiae that can be used to distinguish families from similar groups, the fact that some of these similar groups now consider themselves families necessitates a re-evaluation of the differentiae.

The two most distinctive and often problematic features of a lesbian family are that both parents are female and that the relationship between them is homosexual. These two factors do not necessarily go hand in hand (two women could co-parent without being lesbian), but when they do they relegate lesbian families to a particular social fate. Elena DiLapi (1989) offers an insightful analysis of the social position that lesbian families occupy. She argues that there is a 'motherhood hierarchy' that reflects the different valuations assigned to mothers, primarily on the basis of their family forms. According to DiLapi:

Sexual orientation and family form are the primary criteria for placement on the hierarchy and affect the judgement of who is appropriate for motherhood. Fertility status, method of achieving pregnancy/parenthood, and decision to parent influence one's placement on the hierarchy.

This motherhood hierarchy operates through formal and informal social policy. Ultimately it determines who has access to reproductive health care and parenthood. Those who fit the 'appropriate mother' stereotype have the greatest access to information and resources to parent. (108)

At the top of the motherhood hierarchy are married, middle-class, heterosexual women who are part of a nuclear family. In the middle are heterosexual women who are single, poor, or adolescent. At the bottom are lesbian mothers, who not only are regarded as the least suitable mothers, but also receive the least attention from social agencies and policy-makers.

DiLapi contends that one's placement in the hierarchy is determined by one's *sexual orientation* and *family status*. Yet this ranking can also be explained in terms of a woman's *emotional and relational proximity* to, or her *intimacy* with, a middle-class male. The woman at the top is more or less intimately attached to a middle-class heterosexual male. The woman in the middle may be intimately attached to a male, but either he is not middle class or she is not married to him. At the bottom of the hierarchy is the lesbian woman who has no intimate relationship with a middle-class heterosexual male.

What these three criteria suggest is that a woman is evaluated as a mother less on the basis of her own merits than on the basis of the social position of the father and the relationship she has with him. In this sense, lesbian motherhood can be seen as a truly subversive activity that poses more than a mere conceptual threat. Contrary to popular myth, lesbianism is not fundamentally a response to or rejection of men. It has relatively little to do with men. Lesbians are not so much women-without-men as they are women-with-women. Apart from having to live in a patriarchal society and associate with certain male friends and relatives, men are often truly irrelevant in lesbian lives. This is more than a conceptual threat; it is a structural threat to patriarchal power in Canadian society. A subculture of women is not only living with little regard for males and male authority, but its members are also reproducing themselves! Moreover, they are doing so, as much as possible, without men. It is no wonder that the women in my sample observed so much distress on the part of others over the absence of a male role model in the house.

The lesbian subculture is not the only subculture to which lesbian mothers belong. As we have seen, they are also members of the more general maternal subculture. What appears to be of utmost importance in determining whether a woman is 'really' a mother is whether she has given birth. Although a woman's marital status, socio-economic status, and sexual orientation may influence how other mothers evaluate her mothering, if she has given birth it is accepted that she *is* a mother. But once again, lesbians pose a challenge. The blended-family mothers tend to 'fight it out' in their homes as the stepmother tries to establish some sort of maternal role and the biological mother often hesitates to relinquish maternal authority or share the title 'mother.' For the D.I. mothers, the battle occurs elsewhere. Inside the home, they are both 'mother,' equally sharing the role, label, and authority. But outside the home, and within the maternal culture, only one of them – the biological mother – is considered the 'real' mother. The non-biological mother is often dismissed as a presumptuous interloper. However, this situation is unacceptable to D.I. mothers, and as more lesbian women pursue motherhood by this means – thereby increasing the visibility of the D.I. family form – and demand to be acknowledged as mothers, the educative effect may be such that *all* mothers will come to rethink what it means to be a mother.

It should be clear by now that the lesbian family is not merely an anomalous, ephemeral social entity that we should 'tolerate.' Rather, it is a revolutionary force in our understanding of motherhood and the family – a force that has implications for family-focused policies and programs. It does not appear that lesbian families are going to disappear. Every woman I spoke with in the course of my research knew of several others who were either considering how to go about having children or had started the insemination process. As mainstream assistance (e.g., fertility clinics) becomes more widely available, we can reasonably expect the numbers of lesbian mothers and families to increase, perhaps dramatically.

With respect to future studies of lesbian families, several avenues remain unexplored. One of the most obvious of these concerns the perspectives of the children. We cannot hope to have a completely accurate view of life in lesbian families if we fail to speak with the children who live within them. Because the focus of my study was on reproductive decision-making, mothering, and family life from the perspective of the mothers, I did not pursue this line of inquiry. Informal discussions with some of the children, however, made me regret that I did not have the time to include them.

One theme that emerged in the majority of my interviews was that of the 'dysfunctional family.' Many of my respondents said that their families of origin were dysfunctional, a claim that is certainly not unique to lesbian women. Many of the women told me that they were making a conscious effort to avoid repeating history with their own children. Although I did not have the time to pursue this issue, it would be worthwhile to study how both heterosexuals and homosexuals define for themselves 'dysfunctional' and 'functional' families, and to explore how they are trying to create the latter.

Another possible area of research is the 'culture of motherhood.' I am convinced that research into the mothers' subculture will reveal a previously overlooked dimension of motherhood and give us further insight into the types of power possessed by women, especially mothers. We might also learn more about the social spaces that women occupy, and thus about the perspectives that women have on the society at large.

I have discovered in the course of my research that one can learn much about 'the family' by examining its alternative forms as well as its conventional one. The growth in the number of alternative families – whether lesbian, gay, or single-parent – will require sociologists, feminists, and laypersons to reassess their views on what it means to be a family, to be a mother or a father. They may discover, as the women in this study demonstrate, that things are not always what they seem.

Appendix 1

General Interview Guide[1]

I. THE COUPLE

A. Demographic Information
- ages
- income bracket
- occupations
- education
- length of time together

B. Individual Family Backgrounds
- size/structure of family of origin
- parental roles/role models
- parents' attitudes re:
  - female roles
  - lesbianism
  - this relationship
  - idea of lesbian parenting
  - this child/attempt/decision-making process

C. Division of Labour within Relationship
- occupations/roles
- decision-making

D. Self-Definitions
- as individuals/women/lesbians
- as couple

---

1 Section I is addressed to all respondents, sections II–V primarily to D.I. couples, and section VII – as its heading states – to blended families.

II. THE DECISION-MAKING PROCESS

A. The Biological Mother
- where did the idea begin and whose idea was it
- what were the considerations involved
- role in the decision-making process
- how was it decided she would be the mother
- what does it mean to be a mother
    - anticipated nature of motherhood
- what does it mean to want to be a mother
- what were the issues/conflicts and how were they resolved
    - e.g.: - family support
        - social attitudes
            - toward lesbian relationship
            - toward child in lesbian relationship
            - child's social milieu
        - legal risks
- timing and perceptions of pregnancy

B. The Co-Parent
(essentially the same questions as above – rephrased as necessary)
- perception of role
    - what does it mean to 'mother' but not give birth
- why did she want this
    - what did she want
    - who wanted what
- what were the considerations involved
- role in the decision-making process
- how was it decided that the partner would 'mother'
- what is her role/anticipated role
    - what term does she use to describe role
    - what does it mean to 'co-parent'
    - what does it mean to want to co-parent
- issues/questions/conflicts that had to be addressed/resolved
    - how were they resolved
    - e.g.: - attitudes of family and partner's family towards her role
        - social attitudes
            - towards relationship
            - towards child
        - legal risks

– absence of legal claim to child in the event of separation
– timing of pregnancy

III. THE IMPREGNATION/ACQUISITION

– procedure employed
– each partner's role/experience with the procedure
  – what were each person's experience/feelings/thoughts/perceptions when it came right down to doing it
  – effect of procedure on perceptions of body/role/motherhood
  – difficulties/frustrations with the method
    – were they taken into consideration when the original decision was made
    – how were these handled
  – benefits of this method

IV. THE PREGNANCY

– effect on relationship/dynamics
– each person's role
– perceptions of this time
  – how did the pregnant one feel about being pregnant
  – what were the co-parent's feelings about partner's pregnancy and own non-pregnancy
  – did new issues arise that were not considered/anticipated when the decision was originally made
  – perceptions/definitions of relationship from:
    – selves
    – families
    – lesbian community
    – friends
    – co-workers

V. THE BIRTH

– each partner's account/experience of the birth
– family/friend/community response
– where did the birth take place
  – was partner present
  – partner's access to mother and child
  – staff attitudes

VI. THE EXPERIENCES WITH THE CHILD

- effect on couple dynamics
- with family/friends/community
- roles/division of labour
- definitions/perceptions
    - own
    - those of others

VII. BLENDED FAMILIES

- considerations getting into family/relationship
- social support
- role of both women
    - domestic
    - parenting
- who are you to the children
- children's responses
- issues and concerns
- benefits
- how are they presented in the public world

Appendix 2

Resources for Lesbian Mothers

1. SUPPORT/SOCIAL GROUPS

The names of lesbian mothers'/gay parents' groups across Canada are provided below, along with basic information about each group. The absence of a listing for any given district is due to my inability to locate or contact a group in that area, and should not necessarily be taken to indicate that a group does not exist in the district. Many urban centres in Canada operate lesbian and gay telephone information lines or are home to social/support groups. For those looking for a local parenting group, these are good places to start.

Representatives of some of the gay/lesbian community groups that I contacted indicated that, although there was no formal parents' group in the area, they had members who were parents and who would be interested in meeting other parents. Women's and alternative book stores may provide information about groups and events.

Most local lesbian/gay phone lines and support groups are listed in the local telephone directory. A useful national resource is *The Bent Guide to Gay/Lesbian Canada* (Toronto: Bent Books and ECW Press, 1994).

British Columbia

Vancouver: Community Action for Lesbian Mothers
- meets every Friday 7:00–9:00 p.m. at Eastside Family Place, Brittania Community Centre (at Grandview and Commercial Drive)
- for further information, call the Vancouver Gay-Lesbian Switchboard at (604) 684-6869 or (604) 684-5307 (Mon. to Fri. 7:00–10:00 p.m.)

Alberta

Calgary: Lesbian Mothers' Support Society
- for information call the Lesbian Information Line, (403) 265-9458 (Mon. and Wed. 7:30–9:30 p.m.)
- 211, 223-12 Avenue S.W., Calgary, AB

Edmonton: Lesbian Mothers Network
- contact Anne Erskine at (403) 437-4055
- primarily a support group offering some independently organized social activities

Red Deer: Gay and Lesbian Association of Central Alberta (GALACA)
- a social/support organization for lesbian women and gay men
- several members are parents
- mailing address: GALACA, Box 1078, Red Deer, AB t4n 6s5
- (403) 340-2198 (24-hour answering machine)

Grande Prairie: The Peace Gay Association
- there is no established lesbian mothers' group, but for name of contact person call the Peace Gay Association at (403) 539-3325 (Tues. to Sat. 7:30–9:30 p.m.)

Saskatchewan

Saskatoon: Gay and Lesbian Parent Group of Saskatoon
- a support and social group
- contact Randy at (306) 343-6087
- for further information, contact Gay and Lesbian Health Services at (306) 665-1224

Ontario

Kingston: Lesbian and Gay Parents with Children in the School System
- meetings at Beechgrove Children's Centre, 798 King Street West, Room 226
- for information on meeting dates and times, call the Lesbian/Gay Association at (613) 545-2960 (Mon. to Fri. 7:00–9:00 p.m.; 24-hour answering machine)

Ottawa: Ottawa Lesbian Parents Group
- a social group that meets monthly and organizes events for parents and children
- contact Suzanne at (613) 821-4652

Toronto: Children of Lesbians and Gays Everywhere (COLAGE)
- newsletter, pen pals, kids club, etc.
- COLAGE, Box 187, Station F, Toronto, ON M4Y 2L5

Gay and Lesbian Parents Coalition
- (416) 925-9872, extension 2103 (recorded message)

Gay and Lesbian Parents Coalition International
- P.O. Box 187, Station F, Toronto, ON M4Y 2L5

Quebec

Montreal: Association des Mères Lesbiennes de Montréal
- contact Madeleine Boucher at (514) 725-0078
- primarily French-speaking support group for lesbian mothers offering discussions and some social activities

Centre Communautaire des Gays et Lesbiennes de Montréal (CCGLM)
- services in French, resources, reference centre
- for information on events and groups, call (514) 528-8424

Prince Edward Island

Charlottetown: Lesbian Collective
- no mothers' group, but there are lesbian mothers in the collective
- for name of contact person, call (902) 566-9733 (Wed. 7:00–10:00 p.m.).

United States

Momazons
- a national organization and referral network by and for lesbians choosing children
- bimonthly interactive newsletter
- for sample newsletter and membership information, send US$3.00 to Momazons, P.O. Box 02069, Columbus, OH 43202
- phone: (614) 267-0193

Lavender Families Resource Network
- formerly the Lesbian Mothers' National Defense Fund
- contact information for parents' and children's support groups, quarterly newsletter, and many other services
- for more information, write to Lavender Families Resource Network, Box 21567, Seattle, WA 98111 or call (206) 325-2643

2. NEWSLETTERS

GLPCI Network
- newsletter of the Gay and Lesbian Parents Coalition International
- mailing address: GLPCI, c/o Gay Fathers of Toronto, Box 187, Station F, Toronto, ON M4Y 2L5

The Family Next Door
- national bimonthly publication for lesbian and gay parents and their friends
- for a free copy, write to Next Door Publishing, P.O. Box 21580, Oakland, CA 94620
- phone/fax: (510) 482-5778

3. BOOKS FOR CHILDREN

In recent years there has been a vast increase in the publication of books that are lesbian/gay positive or written specifically for children in lesbian/gay families. There are, in fact, too many titles to list here. Local women's, university, and alternative book stores can provide assistance in locating individual titles. The following resources should also be helpful.

Annotated bibliography of over eighty-five picture books for children (birth to age eleven) of gay and lesbian parents
- send US$2.50 to GLPCI, P.O. Box 43206, Montclair, NJ 07043
- available from the same address is *Bibliography on Gays and Lesbians and Their Families* (cost: US$5.00)

Joined by Love: A Book Catalog for Lesbian and Gay Families
- available through Tapestry Books, P.O. Box 359, Ringoes, NJ 08551–0359
- phone: (908) 806-6695/ fax: (908) 788-2999

4. FILMS/VIDEOS

There are numerous films and videos dealing with various aspects of lesbian/gay family life that you should be able to track down with a little persistence. A useful starting place might be your local branch office of the National Film Board. Also watch for local gay and lesbian film festivals, which many communities include in their Gay and Lesbian Pride Week celebrations. Another useful contact is the Gay and Lesbian Parents Coalition International (P.O. Box 187, Station F, Toronto ON M4Y 2L5). This group has recently released a video and accompanying handbook entitled *Both of My Moms' Names are Judy: Children of*

Lesbians and Gays Speak Out. To order a copy of this video, send US$25 to GLPCI, P.O. Box 43206, Montclair, NJ 07043.

Listed below are the names and addresses of film distributers that specialize in lesbian/gay films and videos:

V-Tape
    401 Richmond Street West, Suite 452,
    Toronto, ON M5V 3A8
    phone: (416) 351-1317
    fax: (416) 351-1509

Canadian Filmmakers Distribution West
    1131 Howe Street, Suite 100,
    Vancouver, BC V6Z 2L7
    phone: (604) 684-3014
    fax: (604) 684-7165

Canadian Filmmakers Distribution Centre
    67A Portland Street,
    Toronto, ON M5V 2M9
    phone: (416) 593-1808
    fax: (416) 593-8661

Video Out Distribution
    1965 Main Street
    Vancouver, BC V5T 3C1
    phone: (604) 688-8449
    fax: (604) 876-1185

First Run/Icarus Films
    153 Waverly Place, sixth floor,
    New York City, NY 10014
    phone: (212) 727-1711
    fax: (212) 989-7649

Frameline
    346 Ninth Street
    San Francisco, CA 94103
    phone: (415) 703-8654
    fax: (415) 861-1404

Bibliography

LESBIAN MOTHERING/LESBIAN FAMILIES

Allen, Katherine R., and David H. Demo. 'The Families of Lesbians and Gay Men: A New Frontier in Family Research.' *Journal of Marriage and the Family* 57, no. 1 (February 1995): 111–28.

Alpert, Harriet, ed. *We Are Everywhere: Writings by and about Lesbian Parents.* Freedom, CA: Crossing Press, 1988.

Arnup, Kathy. 'Lesbian Mothers and Child Custody.' In Arlene Tigar McLaren, ed., *Gender and Society.* Toronto: Copp Clark, 1988.

– 'Mothers Just like Others: Lesbians, Divorce and Child Custody in Canada.' *Canadian Journal of Women and the Law* 3 (1989): 18–32.

– 'We Are Family: Lesbian Mothers in Canada.' *Resources for Feminist Research* 20, nos. 3/4 (1991): 101–7.

– *Lesbian Parenting: Living with Pride and Prejudice.* Charlottetown: Gynergy Books, 1995.

Benkov, Laura. *Reinventing the Family: The Emerging Story of Lesbian and Gay Parents.* Ithaca, NY: Cornell University Press, 1993.

Bozett, Frederick W., ed. *Gay and Lesbian Parents.* New York: Praeger, 1987.

Burke, Phyllis. *Family Values: A Lesbian Mother's Fight for Her Son.* New York: Random House, 1993.

Corley, Rip. *The Final Closet.* Miami: Editech Press, 1990.

Crawford, Sally. 'Lesbian Families: Psychosocial Stress and the Family-Building Process.' In *Lesbian Psychologies*, edited by the Boston Lesbian Psychologies Collective, 195–214. Chicago: University of Illinois Press, 1987.

Day, Dian. 'Lesbian/Mother.' In Sharon Dale Stone, ed., *Lesbians in Canada.* Toronto: Between the Lines, 1990.

DiLapi, Elena Marie. 'Lesbian Mothers and the Motherhood Hierarchy.' *Journal of Homosexuality* 18, nos. 1/2 (1989): 101–21.

Dineen, Claire, and Jackie Crawford. 'Lesbian Mothering.' *Fireweed* 28 (Spring 1989): 24–35.

Gross, Wendy. 'Judging the Best Interests of the Child: Child Custody and the Homosexual Parent.' *Canadian Journal of Family and the Law* 1 (1986): 505–31.

Hanscombe, Gillian, and Jackie Forster. *Rocking the Cradle: Lesbian Mothers, a Challenge in Family Living.* Boston: Alyson Publications, 1982.

Hunter, Nan D. 'Custody Rights of Lesbian Mothers: Legal Theory and Litigation Strategy.' *Buffalo Law Review,* 25, no. 3 (Spring 1976): 691–733.

Kirkpatrick, M., C. Smith, and R. Roy. 'Lesbian Mothers and Their Children: A Comparative Survey.' *American Journal of Orthopsychiatry* 51: 545–51.

Lambda Legal Defense and Education Fund, Inc. *Lesbians Choosing Motherhood: Legal, Medical, and Social Issues.* New York, 1984.

Levy, Eileen F. 'Lesbian Motherhood: Identity and Social Support.' *Affilia* 4, no. 4 (Winter 1989): 40–53.

Lewin, Ellen. *Lesbian Mothers: Accounts of Gender in American Culture.* New York: Cornell University Press, 1993.

– 'Negotiating Lesbian Motherhood: The Dialectics of Resistance and Accommodation.' In Evelyn Nakano Glenn, Grace Chang, and Linda Rennie, eds, *Mothering: Ideology, Experience, and Agency.* New York: Routledge, 1994.

Liljesfraund, Petra. 'Children without Fathers: Handling the Anonymous Donor Question.' *Out/Look* (Fall 1988): 24–9.

Lorde, Audre. 'Turning the Beat Around: Lesbian Parenting 1986.' In Audre Lorde, *A Burst of Light.* Toronto: Women's Press, 1988.

Loulan, JoAnn. 'Sex and Motherhood.' In JoAnn Loulan, *Lesbian Sex,* 159–78. San Francisco: Spinster's Ink, 1984.

MacPike, Loralee, ed. *There's Something I've Been Meaning to Tell You.* Tallahassee, FL: Naiad Press, 1989.

Martin, April. *Lesbian and Gay Parenting Handbook: Creating and Raising Our Families.* New York: Harper Perenial, 1993.

McBride, Hugh. 'Two Mommies and a Mortgage.' *The Financial Post Magazine,* October 1994, 56–9.

Miller, Judith Ann, R. Brooke Jacobsen, and Jerry J. Bigner. 'The Child's Home Environment for Lesbian vs. Heterosexual Mothers: A Neglected Area of Research.' *Journal of Homosexuality* 7, no. 1 (Fall 1981): 49–56.

O'Brien, Carol Anne, and Lorna Weir. 'Lesbians and Gay Men inside and outside Families.' In Nancy Mandell and Ann Duffy, eds; *Canadian Families: Diversity, Conflict and Change,* 111–40. New York: Harcourt Brace and Co., 1995.

Pagelow, Mildred D. 'Heterosexual and Lesbian Single Mothers: A Comparison of Problems, Coping, and Solutions.' *Journal of Homosexuality* 5, no. 3 (Spring 1980): 189–204.

Pies, Cheri. *Considering Parenthood*. San Francisco: Spinsters/Aunt Lute, 1988.

Pollack, Sandra, and Jeanne Vaughn, eds. *Politics of the Heart: A Lesbian Parenting Anthology*. Ithaca, NY: Firebrand Books, 1987.

Rafkin, Louise, ed. *Different Mothers: Sons and Daughters of Lesbians Talk about Their Lives*. San Francisco: Cleis Press, 1990.

Robson, Ruthann. 'Mother: The Legal Domestication of Lesbian Existence.' *Hypatia* 7, no. 4 (Fall 1992): 172–85.

Shapiro, Donald E., and Lisa Schultz. 'Single-Sex Families: The Impact of Birth Innovations upon Traditional Family Notions.' *Journal of Family Law* 24 (1985–6): 271–81.

Stone, Sharon Dale. 'Lesbian Mothers Organizing.' In Sharon Dale Stone, ed., *Lesbians in Canada*. Toronto: Between the Lines, 1990.

Vermeulen, K. 'A Family Comes Out.' *Out/Look* (Spring 1991): 46–8.

Wallace, Mary, Lee MacKay, and Dorrie Nagler. *Children and Feminism*. Vancouver: The Lesbian and Feminist Mothers Political Action Group, 1987.

Weston, Kath. *Families We Choose: Lesbians, Gays, Kinship*. New York: Columbia University Press, 1991.

SELF/DONOR INSEMINATION

Adamson, Nancy. 'Self-Insemination.' *Healthsharing* (Fall 1985): 8–9.

Coffey, Mary Anne. 'Of Father Born: A Lesbian Feminist Critique of the Ontario Law Reform Commission Recommendations on Artificial Insemination.' *Canadian Journal of Women and the Law* 1, no. 2 (1986): 424–33.

– 'Seizing the Means of Reproduction: Proposal for an Exploratory Study of Alternative Fertilization and Parenting Strategies among Lesbian Women.' *Resources for Feminist Research* 18, no. 3 (1989): 76–9.

Ledward, R.S., L. Crawford, and E.M. Symonds. 'Social Factors in Patients for Artificial Insemination by Donor (AID).' *Journal of Biosocial Science* 11: 473–9.

Lesbian Health Information Project. *Artificial Insemination for Lesbians and Gay Men*. San Francisco, n.d.

McGuire, M., and N. Alexander. 'Artificial Insemination of Single Women.' *Fertility and Sterility* 43: 182–4.

Perkoff, Gerald T. 'Artificial Insemination in a Lesbian: A Case Analysis.' *Archives of Internal Medicine* 145 (March 1985): 527–31.

Saffron, Lisa. *Getting Pregnant Our Own Way: A Guide to Alternative Insemination*. London: Women's Health Information Centre, 1986.

San Francisco Women's Center. *Artificial Insemination: An Alternative Conception.* San Francisco, n.d.

Stern, Susan. 'Lesbian Insemination.' *The Coevolution Quarterly* (Summer 1980): 108–17.

Swanbrow, Diane. 'Immaculate Conceptions.' *New West* 25 (August 1980): 27–31.

Walker, Robert. 'Fertility Service Won't Bar Singles.' *Calgary Herald*, November 3, 1990, B1.

REPRODUCTIVE DECISION-MAKING

Currie, Dawn. 'Rethinking What We Do and How We Do It: A Study of Reproductive Decisions.' *Canadian Review of Sociology and Anthropology* 25, no. 2 (1988): 231–53.

Pies, Cheri. *Considering Parenthood.* San Francisco: Spinsters/Aunt Lute, 1988.

Rowland, Robyn. 'Technology and Motherhood: Reproductive Choice Reconsidered.' *Signs* 12, no. 3 (1987): 512–28.

Silka, Linda, and Sara Kiesler. 'Couples Who Choose to Remain Childless.' *Family Planning Perspectives* 9, no. 1 (January/February 1977): 16–25.

LESBIAN LIVES

Andrews, Nancy. *Family: A Portrait of Gay and Lesbian America.* San Francisco: Harper, 1994.

Barrett, Martha Barron. *Invisible Lives.* New York: Harper and Row, 1990.

Bell, A.P., and M.S. Weinberg. *Homosexualities: A Study of Diversity among Men and Women.* New York: Simon and Schuster, 1978.

Berzon, Betty, ed. *Positively Gay.* Los Angeles: Mediamix Associates, 1979.

Fairchild, Betty, and Nancy Hayward. *Now That You Know.* New York: Harcourt Brace Jovanovich, 1979.

Goodman, Gerre, George Lakey, Judy Lashoff, and Erika Thorne. *No Turning Back: Lesbian and Gay Liberation for the 80s.* Philadelphia: New Society Publishers, 1983.

Herman, Didi. *Rights of Passage: Struggles for Lesbian and Gay Legal Equality.* Toronto: University of Toronto Press, 1994.

Hughes, Nym, Yvonne Johnson, and Yvette Perreault. *Stepping Out of Line: A Workbook on Lesbianism and Feminism.* Vancouver: Press Gang Publishers, 1984.

Jackson, Ed, and Stan Persky, eds. *Flaunting It!* Vancouver: New Star Books, 1982.

Johnston, Jill. *Lesbian Nation.* New York: Touchstone, 1974.

Kitzinger, Celia. *The Social Construction of Lesbianism*. London: Sage Publications, 1987.

Marmor, Judd, ed. *Homosexual Behaviour*. New York: Basic Books, 1980.

Martin, Del, and Phyllis Lyon. *Lesbian/Woman*. New York: Bantam Books, 1983.

Nichols, Margaret. 'Lesbian Sexuality: Issues and Developing Theory.' In *Lesbian Psychologies*, edited by the Boston Lesbian Psychologies Collective, 97–125. Chicago: University of Illinois Press, 1987.

O'Donnell, M., et al. *Lesbian Health Matters: A Resource Book about Lesbian Health*. Santa Cruz, CA: Santa Cruz Women's Health Collective, 1979.

Rich, Adrian. 'Compulsory Heterosexuality and Lesbian Existence.' In *Powers of Desire: The Politics of Sexuality*, edited by Ann Snitow et al. New York: Monthly Review Press, 1983.

Smith, Elizabeth A. 'Butches, Femmes and Feminists: The Politics of Lesbian Sexuality.' *NWSA Journal* 1, no. 3 (Spring 1989): 398–421.

Stone, Sharon Dale, ed. *Lesbians in Canada*. Toronto: Between the Lines, 1990.

Vida, Ginny, ed. *Our Right to Love*. New Jersey: Prentice Hall, 1978.

Wolf, Deborah Coleman. *The Lesbian Community*. Los Angeles: University of California Press, 1980.

MOTHERING, REPRODUCTION, AND REPRODUCTIVE TECHNOLOGIES

Achilles, Rona. 'New Age Procreation.' *Healthsharing* (Fall 1984): 10–14.

Chodorow, Nancy. *The Reproduction of Mothering*. Berkeley: University of California Press, 1978.

Cisarole, Donna M., and Joni Seager. 'Women and Reproductive Technologies: A Partially Annotated Bibliography.' *Women and Health*, no. 13 (1987): 77–93.

CRIAW. *Reproductive Technologies and Women: A Research Tool*. Ottawa, 1989.

Crowe, Christine. '"Women Want It": In-Vitro Fertilization and Women's Motivations for Participation.' *Women's Studies International Forum* 8, no. 6 (1985): 547–52.

Dye, Nancy Schrom. 'History of Childbirth in America.' *Signs* 6, no. 1 (1980): 97–108.

Gordon, L. *Woman's Body, Woman's Right: A Social History of Birth Control in the U.S.* New York: Viking/Penguin, 1976.

Jagger, Alison M., and William L. McBride. '"Reproduction" as Male Ideology.' *Women's Studies International Forum* 8, no. 3 (1985): 185–96.

Koch, Lee, and Janine Morgall. 'Towards a Feminist Assessment of Reproductive Technology.' *Acta Sociologica* 30, no. 2 (1987): 172–91.

Luxton, Meg, Harriet Rosenberg, and Sedef Arat-Koc. *Through the Kitchen Window*. Toronto: Garamond Press, 1990.

McLaren, Angus, and Arlene McLaren. *The Bedroom and the State: The Changing Practices and Politics of Contraception and Abortion in Canada, 1880–1980*. Toronto: McClelland and Stewart, 1986.

Oakley, Ann. *The Sociology of Housework*. New York: Pantheon, 1974.

– *Housewife*. Harmondsworth: Penguin, 1976.

O'Brien, Mary. *The Politics of Reproduction*. Boston: Routledge and Kegan Paul, 1981.

Overall, Christine. *Ethics and Human Reproduction*. Boston: Allen and Unwin, 1987.

– 'Reproductive Technology and the Future of the Family.' In *Women and Men: Interdisciplinary Readings on Gender*, edited by Greta Hofman Nemiroff, 245–61. Montreal: Fitzhenry and Whiteside, 1987.

– ed. *The Future of Human Reproduction*. Toronto: Women's Press, 1989.

Rothman, Barbara Katz. *Recreating Motherhood*. New York: W.W. Norton and Co., 1989.

Ruddick, Sara. 'Maternal Thinking.' In Joyce Trebilcot, ed., *Mothering: Essays in Feminist Theory*. Totowa, NJ: Rowman and Allanheld, 1983.

St Peter, Christine. 'Feminist Discourse, Infertility and Reproductive Technologies.' *NWSA Journal* 1, no. 3 (Spring 1989): 353–67.

Trebilcot, Joyce, ed. *Mothering: Essays in Feminist Theory*. Totowa, NJ: Rowman and Allanheld, 1983.

Williams, Linda S. 'Motherhood, Ideology, and the Power of Technology: In Vitro Fertilization Use by Adoptive Mothers.' *Women's Studies International Forum* 13, no. 6 (1990): 543–52.

RESEARCH RESOURCES

Aptheker, Bettina. *Tapestries of Life*. Amherst: University of Massachusetts Press, 1989.

Devault, Marjorie L. 'Talking and Listening from Women's Standpoint: Feminist Strategies for Interviewing and Analysis.' *Social Problems* 37, no. 1 (February 1990): 96–115.

Glaser, Barney G., and Anselm L. Strauss. *The Discovery of Grounded Theory: Strategies for Qualitative Research*. New York: Aldine Publishing Company, 1967.

Hawkesworth, Mary E. 'Knowers, Knowing, Known: Feminist Theory and Claims of Truth.' *Signs* 14, no. 3 (1989): 533–57.

La Novara, Pina. 'Changes in Family Living.' *Canadian Social Trends* (Summer 1993): 12–14.

Oderkirk, Jillian, and Clarence Lochhead. 'Lone Parenthood: Gender Differences.' *Canadian Social Trends* (Winter 1992): 16–19.

Smith, Dorothy E. *The Everyday World as Problematic*. Toronto: University of Toronto Press, 1987.

Stebbins, Robert A. *Deviance: Tolerable Differences*. Toronto: McGraw-Hill Ryerson, 1988.

Van Maanen, John. *Tales of the Field*. Chicago: University of Chicago Press, 1988.

Index